Communication in the design process

Communication in the design process

Stephen A. Brown

London and New York

First published 2001 by Spon Press
11 New Fetter Lane, London EC4P 4EE

Simultaneously published in the USA and Canada
by Spon Press
29 West 35th Street, New York, NY 10001

Spon Press is an imprint of the Taylor & Francis Group

Typeset in Gill Sans Light by Wearset, Boldon, Tyne and Wear
Printed and bound in Great Britain by Biddles Ltd, Guildford and King's Lynn

British Library Cataloguing in Publication Data
A catalogue record for this book is available from the British Library

Library of Congress Cataloging in Publication Data
Brown, Stephen A., 1953–
    Communication in the design process / Stephen A. Brown.
        p.   cm.
    Includes bibliographical references and index.
    1. Communication in architectural design–Case studies. 2. Architects and
    patrons–Case studies. 3. Architectural practice–Management–Case studies. I. Title.
NA2750 .B735 2001
721'.068'8–dc21   00-045023

ISBN 0-419-25750-0 (pbk)

AL
NA
2750
B735
2001

Contents

Preface

The design and the construction industry, in the broadest sense, impinges upon most organisations and indeed most individuals. For many years the industry has been subjected to criticism and challenge. As a response countless reports and improvement initiatives have been instigated. As the twenty-first century begins, complaints and dissatisfaction by both Employers and Consultants are not dissimilar to those expressed some 40 years ago.

In the role of both Consultant and Employer, the author has observed much dissatisfaction that should not be tolerated. Most damning, however, is the continuous repetition of the same mistakes. This book is prompted by concern that many current initiatives, although commendable, do not sufficiently examine the underlying causes of the problems. They merely concentrate on the instant 'best' practice solution, that may not be in fact, universally applicable.

The author has over 20 years experience as a Chartered Architect, in private practice, and is currently a Director of The Charter Partnership Ltd and Intraspace Ltd. Parallel experience has been gained as Chairman of an Estates Management Company and MD of a construction and development organisation. A changing world has diversified interests and education to include the fields of project management and facility management.

It is the concept of facility management within the design and construction chain that acted very much as a catalyst to this text. The basis of this book is formed, in part, by research undertaken as an element of a masters degree in facility and environmental management, completed at UCL. The book has taken this basic research as a starting point and expanded areas of practice by reference to case studies and further interviews.

This book considers the gap that can exist between Client expectation and realisation in building projects. It focuses upon the communication interface between the Employer and the Consultant design team, and specifically on the areas of function, finance, timescale and aesthetics. The study undertakes an extensive review of current thinking and guidance on this and peripherally related subjects. New data is obtained from a survey using questionnaires and personal semi-structured interviews. Data is presented graphically, analysed and compared with practice as defined in current literature.

Extensive dissatisfaction, in the areas of finance, timescale and function, is identified. An analysis of perceived reasons and profiles of respondents provide a pattern of weaknesses in current practice. The book concludes with six proposals for possible improvement.

The book aims to inform or remind readers of current thinking and practice as well as opening up discussion on a range of impinging issues that are often ignored. It is anticipated that readers will disagree with some conclusions and wholeheartedly agree with others. It is expected that many, although endorsing proposed good practice, will recall, with guilt, recent actions.

The book is intended to appeal to a wide range of readers. It is anticipated there will be practitioners and Employers keen to implement some practical methodology to achieving improvement initiatives. It is also anticipated there will be students or more newly qualified professionals who seek to understand some of the key problems in practice, hopefully with the intention of avoiding some of the pitfalls.

It may be that there is a temptation to turn to the final chapter, and to assimilate quickly improvement strategies for the future. This would be unfortunate and falls into the trap of many of the published guidance documents that are readily available. It is believed that the web of impinging issues and the underlying causation of problems are the key, if future strategies are to be understood, meaningfully interpreted and subsequently implemented. It is hoped therefore that readers will assimilate the background of academic and practice-based thought and comment before judging or, indeed, initiating any of the proposed strategies.

Acknowledgements

A text combining academic thought and practice-based research demands the support of a wide range of people. I thank UCL staff, in particular Bev Nutt, David Kincaid and Peter McLennan for the kernel of the idea and numerous thoughts, debates and soundings.

Without question, the input from the 100 organisations involved in the original research, was invaluable. Indeed without all of the honest and willing responses, the research would have withered. In particular I am indebted to those organisations that committed to the extended interview process.

A wide range of references are used to demonstrate the breadth of existing academic thinking and research. To each, I am grateful, and I acknowledge their contribution to the development of the subject.

I am equally grateful for the indulgence of my office colleagues, and finally, thankful to my wife Else, and daughters Sarah and Anna who provided great support.

1 Introduction

The context

The development of the global village has heightened the people's awareness of communication, particularly across different cultures and languages. Significant efforts in terms of time and technology have been expended in resolving potential misunderstandings, and indeed the world of governmental diplomacy has been founded upon this task. At a daily level the effects of standard protocols are familiar to all in terms of ISO (International Standards Organisation) standards, computer file formats, standard methods of measurement and countless rules and regulations.

It is therefore with some incredulity that one perceives persistent failures to communicate appropriately within cultures and even within a single industry. Communication has been cited by 25 per cent of all construction employers as a basic reason for failure. The same source (Franks 1998, p. 62) refers to these communication problems as being due, in the words of the now aged 1962 Emmerson report, to the 'divorce of design from production'. Current research simply reinforces this finding.

The construction industry, even in its current form, is certainly mature and yet both the popular and the professional view sees major problems in the simplest of tasks. The time that has been expended on the production of systems of control, quality assurance, building contracts and documentation still fails to ease the superficially simple task of communicating. There remain a range of barriers to this most basic of actions. Simple failures to understand the other party at a verbal level stand alongside the baggage of agendas that virtually demands misunderstanding as a commercial negotiating tool.

It is optimistically believed that the current and genuine development of partnership and 'team spirit' is reducing what were extensive departments of 'claims surveyors'. Although there may be fewer people involved in actively seeking out the 'grey' areas for commercial advantage, there still remains plenty of opportunity for completely innocent misinterpretation.

This book is aimed at all those involved with construction, but takes the Client perspective as its primary focus. The academic basis of the author's original research work allowed questions to be asked of Employers that would rarely be broached by a Consultant or Contractor. The combination of practice-based data with academic research and review provides a thought provoking and comprehensive overview of the complex and critical subject.

Best practice within the construction industry demands that Employers, Consultants and Contractors alike obtain feedback and assessment of performance. The reality, however, is that in a small number of cases when feedback actually occurs, it is restricted and often misses the point. Certainly in projects where there are clear problems, most contributors are more than happy to see the conclusion of the project; few wish to embark on opening up issues for which they themselves may be at fault. Long-term relationships, or 'partnering' as it is now popularly called, requires honesty to understand the real feelings and objectives of all parties involved with the project. Interviews with Consultants and Employers regarding case studies have demonstrated little real transparent honesty, although both parties happily confided what, in their opinion, contributes to a problem. Both parties, however, still approached it from different sides, and neither party had openly discussed the particular key issues that were raised with the author. It is the intention of this book to provide an objective overview of 'expectation and realisation'. Each party may find themselves being criticised at some point, but both Employer and Consultant should expect to work together for a common goal if a performance gap is to be closed. Balance is provided by input from a wide range of Consultants, Employers and Contractors, ensuring that all parties within the design process find a perspective appropriate to them.

Most readers will recognise design team scenarios where the Employer is represented by its staff, and Consultants by discipline, both of which frequently change over time. Who is the Client and who is the Consultant? How do you accommodate the personal crusade of the individual that can so easily develop during the life of a project? These issues must be resolved at the earliest stage.

The issues of the multi-headed Client are described in later chapters. The major differences that can occur within an Employer's organisation, and within that of the Consultant, serve only to compound difficulties of communication as multiple agendas and levels of expertise become evident. Common goals and shared motivation may promote good teamwork, but there is nothing to contribute to the mechanisms that will ensure appropriate translation of Employers' requirements into appropriate response. The adequacy of this translation process depends on the interfaces between those involved at project team level, and on the development of appropriate tools to allow this process to occur.

The conclusions of this book are based upon research work carried out by the author during 1998. A high level of questionnaire response, combined with extensive use of interviews and case studies, provides a unique insight into the views of the Employer and the Consultant.

The subject – breadth and depth

A building project, of whatever nature, creates a number of transient communication interfaces. Identification of these interfaces, and their relationship to the nature of the communication gap between expectation and realisation, is essential.

Many otherwise commendable studies and guides fail adequately to address this most fundamental of issues. This book focuses on building projects with the associated Employer and Consultant team that is invariably formed.

During the 1980s several sources identified that a gap does indeed exist between expectation and realisation. Parasuraman (Parasuraman *et al.* 1985), researched the issues of customer satisfaction in the USA. Their work concluded that there were five gaps in the provision of service between customer and provider. These gaps were not identified in the context of the construction industry but, nevertheless, form the basis of the consideration of the Employer and Consultant/Contractor in the respective roles of 'the customer and provider'. These were later expanded upon by the RIBA (1993, p. 11) and Usmani and Winch (1993, p. 29), to be directly relevant to the construction industry, and have subsequently formed the foundations for much speculative research in the industry in the pursuit of 'improvement'. The identification of these gaps acts as the base for the consideration of 'formative factors' and, as such, a precursor to the proposal of any strategies for improvement. It is suggested that, without careful consideration and understanding of the impinging issues, and of these 'formative factors', strategies alone will become misguided or simply misunderstood.

Numerous parallel surveys (Walker 1989, p. 71; Barrett and Males 1991, p. 176; Becker 1991, p. 192) indicate significant dissatisfaction with building projects, on the part of both the Employer and the Occupant. The latter already begins to expand the subject. The difference between Employer and Occupant is enormous. Are either, neither or both Clients? Many Occupants may as yet be unknown or indeed unborn. It is clear, however, that current relationships between flesh-and-blood Employers and their Consultants/Contractors continue to lead to disputes.

This problem is exacerbated by the ever increasing level of litigation within the construction industry. Despite the attitude shift referred to previously in terms of demise of the claims department, extended legal wrangles are still commonplace. The Construction Act 1997 included provisions to reduce the quantity of high level litigation between contracting parties. However, the immediate result has been an explosion of minor formalised legal claims, as contracting parties seek to conclude disputes that would have otherwise resulted in protracted negotiation outside of the law. A recent academic report (Somogyi 1999, 'Summary') identified that 87 per cent of respondents had been involved with a dispute of some kind in the last 5 years. Fortunately the vast majority were resolved by negotiation, but a significant 3 per cent continued up to the High Court.

It is the commencement of the design process that normally brings together a variety of project team members. The fact that they are often complete strangers, both in terms of organisations and individuals, is not without significance. The design process itself is commonly a few centimetres on a bar chart that may be a metre long. Stretching the imagination a little, one can see the traditional design exercise in the life cycle of a facility as much like the existence of man in relation to the existence of life! The effect of this short intervention, however, is significant. Cradle-to-grave involvement would appear more responsible. Design often starts after the strategic decisions have been made, but it is expected to translate a language of demand, despite having little involvement with its development. It is, too often, a continuum starting with conceptual decisions and culminating during the build process with operational and technical design, but usually with little or no feedback.

Recent years have seen the design process merging into the procurement and build programmes, very much as a result of Design and Build. But still there remains a divide between the primary design process, controlled by consultants, and the myriad of secondary designers. The latter, in the form of Sub-contractors/Suppliers, are however, now being clearly acknowledged. They are very much 'designers', and as a consequence are beginning to become exposed to the problems of 'translation'.

Much work (Atkin et al. 1996; Nutt 1988; Preiser 1993; RIBA 1993) during the late 1980s and early 1990s was directed towards the briefing process and the subsequent techniques for managing 'design'. Recent studies (Bicknell 1998) have shown that Architects, for example, still have little involvement with management issues or strategic decision making. Nevertheless they are expected to understand fully the requirements of our multi-headed Employer to provide facilities that complement the long-term business plan and future technological changes!

It is also clear that many projects exhibit minimal input into the critical strategic brief and, with undue haste, efforts are concentrated on the physical brief. It is not suggested, however, that Consultants are specifically excluded from this strategic brief, because simply it rarely exists. Tactical opportunities and opportunism for short-term financial planning are more commonplace than most dare to acknowledge. It will be shown that common practice jumps from problem to solution rapidly and, as a consequence, back to problem again, albeit a different one. More recently, the emphasis has been on construction and the operational or technical level of design. There has been a plethora of documents providing guidance and analysis for this aspect of the process. This runs the risk, however, of ensuring the running of a perfect train service to the wrong station!

1998 saw the publication of the Government Taskforce document *Rethinking Construction*, generally referred to as the 'Egan Report' (DETR 1998). This deals with the construction industry in the broadest sense, observing levels of dissatisfaction and demanding improvement. Many of the issues peripheral to the author's 1998 study, and noted within current literature and research, are acknowledged by Egan. The report proposes somewhat arbitrary targets for improvement, and loosely bases these upon the earlier studies referred to previously. The apparent arbitrary nature of these targets, however, alienated many who would otherwise support the general ideals. This book endeavours to avoid arbitrary goals and concentrates on issues taken directly from the mouths of everyday Employers and Consultants.

This book focuses upon particular criteria within a building project, and specifically ring-fences those items to maintain focus. Earlier studies by a number of sources (Barrett and Males 1991, p. 176; Garvin 1988, p. 171; Preiser 1993, p. 214; Walker 1989, p. 70) identify key Client issues of concern to be function, finance and timescale.

Initial interviews with a sample of Employers confirmed that these three key areas were also of major importance to them. The focus of this publication and the underlying research therefore is based upon this premise.

Employers also have concerns regarding aesthetics, or as it may be seen, consider that they should! As we are considering the built environment and design, it would seem to be inappropriate to ignore this aspect of the process. Therefore, despite a low profile in earlier studies, aesthetics is evaluated to determine its weighting and significance.

The author's 1998 study therefore focused on the issues of:

- Function: space, usability, operation, appropriateness, location;
- Finance: total cost, variation, reliability, reporting;
- Timescale: pre- and post-contract programme, accuracy, resourcing;
- Aesthetics: visual appearance, acceptability, appropriateness.

Building projects are defined as new build, refurbishment or extension. Specialist activities, such as active mechanical and electrical (M and E) systems or Information Technology (IT) systems, are specifically excluded from this study. It should be noted, however, that the subject of M and E installation and design arose regularly in interviews. As levels of sophistication increase, it is not uncommon for M and E systems to approach 50 per cent of any contract in terms of value, and frequently IT systems can exceed construction cost. Dissatisfaction with M and E design normally becomes an issue on completion and relates to non-performance. This is clear evidence of a performance gap between expectation and realisation; it inevitably involves a chain of designers and contractors, all of whom may have contributed to it. Exclusion of M and E systems from the study is simply to ensure focus for data collection, but in no way suggests that this element of a project is less than critical. Indeed a parallel study, based purely on M and E and IT systems, would have much merit but, it is suggested, would have a similar conclusion. The lessons learnt and the experiences recorded regarding the performance gap in more general construction projects are equally relevant to specialist spheres.

The subject of physical workmanship defects and general contracting problems is enormous, and for this reason the study focuses on the relationship between Employer and Consultant. It is acknowledged that works beyond the completion of design are of major significance to an Employer and significantly effect the balance of expectation to realisation, but the great importance of this interface, together with that of Suppliers and Sub-contractors is worthy of separate study. Indeed, the Egan report concentrates on precisely this area, together with the series of best practice publications issued by the Construction Industry Board.

The 1999 Construction Industry Board survey (CIB 1999) indicates that satisfaction levels with both Consultants and Contractors have improved over a 5-year period. It does not, however, quantify the remaining absolute levels of dissatisfaction in relation to the design process. Two further best practice target setting systems were published in 1999 by CIB and BRE. The practical benefit of these systems is considered in relation to the real problems consistently encountered in everyday projects.

Government task forces have formed the basis of a response to issues that span the environment and the construction industry alike. The Urban Task Force, chaired by Lord Rogers, has set an agenda for regeneration and brownfield development throughout the UK. Close to the subject of the design process, a second task force reported in December 1999, in relation to the role of the Architect in the new millennium.

Basis of the 1998 study

Customer satisfaction has remained a major focus of many industries throughout the last decade. The reconciliation of expectation and realisation, whether related to a service or a product, determines the level of satisfaction achieved. Government and industry initiatives have recognised this within construction. Issues relating to customer satisfaction, design and construction quality, future strategies and technological change are forming the agenda for a plethora of coffee table books and marketing publications assembled by Contractors and academic institutes alike. This is not meant as derogatory comment. Clearly the sooner that such issues become popularly recognised, the sooner a real change will be demanded and enabled throughout the construction industry. Most documentation, however, retains a very narrow focus and often avoids the issue of 'hard numbers'.

Expectation is a complex and composite package of objective and subjective criteria. Some are expressed, but many are simply preconceptions. Realisation is the reality; but for many Employers, this realisation is frequently only evident a long time after the design process, in the conceptual sense, is over and often when the physical product is approaching completion.

Research completed by Brown (1998) has shown that typically 10 per cent of all projects are deemed to have failed in some respect before construction begins. It does not suggest that Employers are knowingly allowing defective design to commence on site, but that simply the reality and consequences of a design are not apparent at that point of the process. Similarly, it is not suggested that Consultants or Contractors collude to allow defects, but the facts simply speak for themselves.

The contributors to the author's research included a wide range of Employers and Consultants. Chapter 5 describes in detail the profile of respondents, the methodology and the analyses of the results. Response rates of up to 50 per cent demonstrate the importance given to the issues under discussion. Unusually, parties willing to contribute in the form of interview and case study significantly exceeded the needs of the study. The need for a balanced population demanded a selection procedure, which is a rare occurrence in this field. Concern, interest and almost passion was certainly not in short supply amongst the Employer and Consultant respondents. This was taken as an indicator of the genuine interest in the subject and a desire to close the gap between expectation and realisation.

The survey population included all types of Employers and Consultants. Employers were categorised as follows:

1   'User type', both experienced and inexperienced;
2   Developer;
3   Design and Build Contractor.

The term 'User type Employer' is used throughout the study to describe those Employers who commission design and construction works for their own direct use, for example manufacturers, retailers, health trusts.

The business of the 'Developer' is defined as the procurement of design and construction of facilities on behalf of others, either on a speculative basis or in conjunction with a specific tenant/purchaser. Design and Build (D and B) Contractors can be found as part of the procurement path for either 'User' or Developer Employers. The nature of D and B however is such that the Contractor is frequently an Employer of design teams in a similar way to the other Employer groups. On the basis that some 30 per cent of new build work is procured by D and B, the views of Contractors have been sought, in their role as Employer. A more detailed analysis of the survey population is included in Chapter 5.

Data was collected by the use of structured closed questions in the form of a widely distributed survey questionnaire. This also allowed, and positively encouraged, open comment. Following analysis of these responses, personal interviews on a semi-structured basis were undertaken with a wide spectrum of respondents.

The critical issues of function, finance and timescale involve a variety of subjective and objective criteria, illustrated by Figure 1.1. While aesthetics may initially appear to be purely subjective, it has been seen that the process of communication between Designer and Employer may be objectively assessed and valued.

Responses span a spectrum from hard to soft. Issues of time and finance

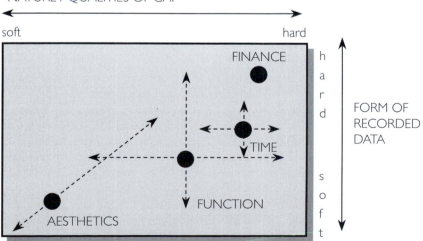

Figure 1.1 Qualities of subject elements

being typically harder measures than issues of function and aesthetics, it was necessary to devise scales to allow for comparison of data at the softer end, together with questions to allow the assessment of weighting. Where subjective terms were used, they were quantified by reference to a percentage or other relevant hard figure.

The summary of the results in subsequent Chapters show the raw figures where appropriate, but generally relates responses on a proportional basis, which is considered more relevant than the use of absolute numerical results. Issues that invited multiple responses at either end of a scale, i.e. common and rare, are represented on single charts with the convention of 'positive' indicating the degree of normality (common) and 'negative' indicating the degree of rarity.

The questionnaire adopted the following form and structure in terms of breadth:

- profile of respondent;
- the project team;
  - composition;
  - leadership;
  - activity level;
  - timing of appointment;
- formation of brief;
  - medium;
  - basis;
- expectation and realisation;
  - failure levels and generic reasons;
  - causation of failure;
- aesthetics;
  - assessment of success;
- open comment.

Simplistically, research covered the issues of who, how and what. It is the 'how' that clearly exposes the weaknesses of current systems, but equally it is the 'how' that is the most difficult issue to address.

Organisation of the text

Although the subject of expectation has been explored extensively in relation to briefing and procedures related to Consultant and Employer communication, there is, with a few notable exceptions, little practical guidance for practitioners that goes beyond traditional linear briefing development routes.

The era since the Latham Report (1994) has seen extensive reference to the 'gaps' noted previously and has focused attention firmly on the brief as a key element in a successful building project. As noted in Chapter 3, the term 'brief' is frequently associated with static documents and linear design processes. 'Information flow' is more appropriate and reference to the 'brief' in this report should be read in this broader context. This book is not about briefing in the absolute sense, but it should be acknowledged that the act of communication, whether it is buying a loaf of bread or procuring a building is, in essence, briefing. It is for this reason that 'briefing' appears to be such a constrained and inadequate term for this act of communication or 'information flow'. Identification of the barriers to good 'flow' and alternative strategies are discussed throughout the text.

Recent years have seen the establishment of facility management (FM) as an independent profession. Its role has been stated as being 'to integrate user interests (demand) and the building team (supply)' (Spedding 1994, p. 76). The potential of this role is significant but, as the 1998 survey and research sources show, facility management retains a low profile at the design stages of most projects. If indeed FM has a role in the design process, this book considers what this is and why it may be beneficial. It also considers why the profile of FM at a strategic level remains low.

This book seeks to derive, from direct communication with Employers and Consultants, together with reference to previous studies, a pattern of how such ideas are being incorporated in to everyday practice. It sets out to re-appraise the question of expectation/realisation in the current context.

The book is organised to consider the scale and nature of the performance gap, who is involved, and why. The web surrounding the subject is explored by reference to past studies and current literature. Past and current views of impinging issues are described and interspersed with evidence and input from the author's study.

The painful facts demonstrated by the study are summarised to provide context and objective fact. These facts are presented in relation to the range of headings described previously, to provide a straight and current view as perceived by Employers and Consultants today.

Clearly many 'alternatives' exist, but how are they viewed? Do they provide real advantage or just 'hot air'. Appropriateness may be the key. Innovation or tradition may be equally counterproductive in the wrong context. The final chapters consider the issues of current practice, available alternative systems and finally strategies to perform beyond current expectations.

The concept of 'best practice' is familiar to both Employer and Consultant and, indeed, in a range of industries. By definition it implies a singular solution. In practice a range of 'good practice' solutions is much preferred. Research suggests that 'emphasis on user pull and local context rather ... than generic best practice' is more appropriate (Barrett and Stanley 1999, pp. 96, 100). The search for the blanket best practice solution can result in as much dissatisfaction as the problem gap itself. The singular ideal of 'best' practice is a myth. Reality shows that the myriad of situations in which both Employer and Consultant find themselves demand a range of 'good' practice solutions.

It is hoped that by combining an overview of current research and literature together with new primary survey data and opinion, this book will inform and stimulate. It is not expected that readers will agree with every proposed strategy, but it is hoped that ideas will be generated and combined with existing practice to actively close the performance gap.

2 What problem?

What problem? Scale and criticality

In order to appreciate the subtlety of the web that surrounds 'expectation and realisation' it is necessary to explore the main issues impinging upon the subject. The next three chapters consider existing supporting work on these issues and provides graphically some of the results of the author's study in the form of raw data, for purposes of clarification and comparison. The sources of the supporting work includes many published and unpublished works, ranging from research projects and surveys to guide books by professional organisations and government. This documentation focuses on the softer fields of psychology, sociology, and management as well as the harder areas of law, finance and professional practice.

The immediate response by many Consultants and Employers acknowledges that improvements may be achievable, but frequently considers that their own systems are acceptable. Even when problems are acknowledged, the root cause is normally alleged to be with another party! In spite of any indignant retorts to the latter statement, it is maintained to be a truth rather than an anecdote. The author's 1998 survey confirmed that Consultants and Employers respond alike in this respect. Chapter 5 expands upon this point and provides the evidence.

The problem therefore needs to be defined. Objective studies by the author and others indicate that a clear gap between expectation and realisation exists. A study by Franks in 1989 (see Franks 1998, p. 60) concluded that 80 per cent of projects could be better. This was not to say that 80 per cent were failures, but that visible room for improvement can clearly be seen in the vast majority of projects. The potential for improvement remains at a similarly high level. The scale and criticality is explored within this chapter; based on the simple Pareto effect (the 80:20 rule) the latter two measures are fundamental.

The relationship is commonplace, it can be objectively analysed for many situations in the relationship shown by Figure 2.1. The old car may have many faults – the heater does not work and the seats are worn – but it performs its primary function until the most minor of engine components fails. The establishment of what is important to both Employers and Consultants is essential. The well used example of the door handle to the chairman's office makes the point but; for example, the ergonomic catastrophe that surrounds each of the production unit work spaces is often ignored. Scale and criticality has to be interpreted in

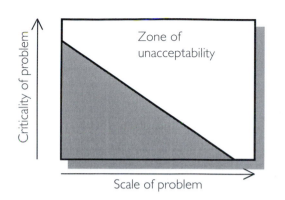

Figure 2.1 Criticality versus scale

relation to power and influence. Stakeholder mapping and user involvement is considered in later chapters.

The plethora of government and construction industry reports and best practice documents are, it is assumed, not produced only to deplete the world's forests, yet few documents quantify the scale of failure in the construction industry. This chapter provides data from the author's own 1998 study and the work of earlier researchers.

Acceptance of the existence of a performance gap, then, demands consideration of:

1   a definition;
2   who is involved?
3   why does the performance gap appear?

Chapters 2, 3 and 4 consider these issues as a series of separate commentaries, providing a range of thoughts that cover both academic and practice based research, as well as some of the results of the 1998 study.

The issues and extent of the problem

Identification – what is it?

The gap between expectation and realisation received little attention until the mid 1980s when Parasuraman investigated the gaps of perception between customers and organisations in relation to service. At a similar time, Total Quality Management systems (TQM) were being developed, prioritising customer focus.

Parasuraman (Parasuraman *et al.* 1985) proposed five service gaps:

Gap 1   Between consumer expectation and management's perception of consumer expectation.
Gap 2   Between management's perception of consumer expectation and

management translations of those perceptions into quality service
specifications

Gap 3   Between service quality specifications and the actual service delivery

Gap 4   Between actual service delivery and external communications about that
service

Gap 5   Between actual service delivery and the consumer's perception of the
service

These relate to 'service' as opposed to the 'communication interface' per se within
a building project context, which is the focus of this book. However, this work
formed the basis of work by the RIBA (1993, p. 11) directly on the gaps between
Client and Architect. The RIBA study expanded these five gaps to describe and
explain gaps between expectation and perception of both Client and Consultant
over a range of issues, including product and, again, service. Obviously the RIBA
study focused on the role of the Architect; however the generic gaps identified
are clearly relevant to the relationship between most construction Consultants
and Employers.

The gaps identified may be summarised as follows.

Gap A – Between Employer's expectation and the Architect's expectation

For the Employer expectations are based upon previous experience or, for
example, discussion with colleagues, or consultant's marketing activities, leading to
a set of expectations. They can relate to personal needs, such as power, job
security, satisfaction, direct involvement, intellectual stimulation, control of risk and
desire to impress. In parallel, organisational expectations will include budget, time,
user requirement and organisational development.

The Architect's expectations are shaped by architectural education, expectations of the profession, personal needs and past experience. From a business perspective there are expectations of revenue generation and external peer approval.

Gap B – Between employer's expectations and his experience of the service

Employers note a lack of trust in Architect's ability to respect cost, time and risk,
and an assumption of leadership. The belief in the Architect's loss of independ-
ence, and poor experiences requiring increased Client knowledge, means later
appointments giving little opportunity to develop the brief. Clients note satisfaction with design work but, as Hayden Davis comments, this is not an effective
counterbalance to problems of time, cost and management.

Gap C – Between Architect's understanding of Employer's expectation and a definition of the service

Provision of standard 'off the peg' services, coupled with a standard form of
appointment, lacks the required subtlety, and creates difficulty in defining the
'value added' of the Architect's service.

Gap D – Between Architect's service specification and the Architect's service delivery

Only part of the services offered are actually supplied, and cost and management as core competencies are rare. As a response, Employers reduce the breadth of requested services in subsequent Architect's appointments.

Gap E – Between the Architect's service delivery and the Employer's perception of the service

There is a subtle gap between the service delivered and the perception of the service, which is dependent upon the quality of the communication. Although the 'magic' supplied by the Architect is valued, non-adherence to constraints of time and budget cannot be ignored and there remains, ultimately, disappointment with the service provided.

Usmani and Winch's (1993, p. 29) later consideration of the gap analysis model identified four main problem areas:

1   the briefing problem, or translation of the Client's requirements into a brief for the project coalition;
2   the design problem, or translation of that brief into the full definition of the proposed building;
3   the execution problem, or the problem of converting that definition into a fully detailed description of the building;
4   the conformance problem of ensuring that the completed building matches that description.

It is primarily gaps 1 and 2 that best describe the thrust of this book. The gap models referred to above are some 10 to 15 years old, yet they effectively set the agenda for the current debate fuelled by government task forces and reports such as that chaired by Egan (DETR 1998).

Quite simply, the project performance gap is the gap between the Employer's expectation and reality. The appropriateness of information flow and the 'transparency' of the interface between Client and Consultant is essential to ensure a process of alignment with expectations. If the 'line of visibility and information flows are opaque then surprises are likely for the client' (Usmani and Winch 1993, p. 29). Despite the Egan agenda there is little real transparency. Too often strategic briefs, where they exist, and certainly project briefs, emerge from under shrouds having been interpreted at face value by Consultants working in isolation.

'The solution' frequently appears from yet more shrouds and is adopted without any true understanding of the implications. The general response evolves into a series of 'catch up' and 'blame' scenarios, as the project bumbles through its life. The team acts like 'a poor player that struts and frets his hour upon the stage, and then is heard no more' (Shakespeare – Macbeth Act 5, Scene 5, lines 24–25).

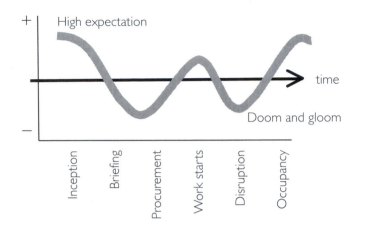

Figure 2.2 Interpretation of doom and gloom rollercoaster
Source: Barrett 1995a, p. 108.

Expectations and goals may change throughout the project, as the knowledge base develops and additional contributors join the project. These changes, however, are more frequently related to an inappropriately developed brief and lack of understanding at inception.

Well publicised diagrams (Barrett 1995a, p. 108) demonstrate the doom and gloom scenarios in projects. The contributors, particularly users, are full of enthusiasm and optimism at the outset, but thereafter their levels of expectation follow a roller coaster (see Figure 2.2). It is also very clear that projects of any significance will often involve a continuous stream of contributors, all of whom may carry the baggage of varying levels of expectation and different agendas.

The issue of agenda is at the very core of 'transparency'. Without an appropriate means of ensuring continuing 'transparency' throughout the life of the project, 'secret' knowledge can develop. The latter can evolve into destructive negative power to aid a personal agenda at the worst or simply, at best, contribute to an expectation gap (see Figure 2.3).

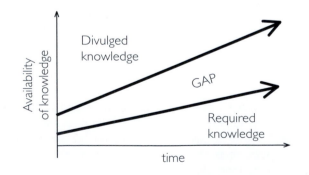

Figure 2.3 Transparency

Critical issues

The primary concerns of Employers have been shown by Hudson Gameson and Murray and the RICS study (Barrett and Males 1991, p. 176) to fall into the primary generic issues of:

- function;
- cost;
- timescale.

Usmani and Winch concluded on the same three factors but noted that 'performance may be assessed in both objective and subjective terms and for some clients not in terms of the finished project but in the method of achieving it' (Usmani and Winch 1993, p. 15).

This is a critical definition. The 'how' is so often overlooked as emphasis is placed upon physical 'deliverables'. Current best practice is bringing the 'how' into the foreground. It is not long ago that the Ministry of Defence defined the 'deliverables' very much in hard terms, yet they are now seen as leading the Egan culture. The issue of 'how' as opposed to 'what' is further explored in Chapter 7, together with the role of the Ministry of Defence in these 'new' initiatives.

Walker (1989, p. 70) quantified his survey work by means of weightings indicating importance to the Client. Where Client objective is 100 per cent, he concluded the following breakdown:

- Quality: 45 per cent (technical standards 15 per cent; functional standards 25 per cent; aesthetic standards 5 per cent);
- Price: 35 per cent (capital costs 25 per cent; life cycle costs 10 per cent);
- Time: 20 per cent.

Work by the University of Reading (Preiser 1993, p. 435) identified similar issues, in addition noting the increasing importance of environmental issues, i.e. planning.

The author's 1998 findings generally agreed but identified aesthetics as having a higher profile, although clearly a lower quantum. Respondent groups were consistent in emphasising the critical importance of failures under the function (31 per cent), finance (30 per cent) and timescale brief (27 per cent), but added aesthetics with a 12 per cent weighting. Figure 2.4 graphically shows the primary concerns of Employers, in terms of potential failures. There is a remarkable correlation with Walker's figures, which demonstrates that, despite a wide variety of initiatives and a much increased profile of the 'brief' that at the end of the century, Employers still have the same distribution of concerns as they did some 20 years earlier.

Timescale is generally a 'hard-edged' issue, measurable against a predetermined programme and against the failure or success of a project. The reality is clearly more subtle and complex. The consequences of timescale failure can range from minor inconvenience to major disaster. Examples likely to fall into the latter category include the retail development required for Christmas trading. At the other extreme the external redecoration of a facility may well only be a minor

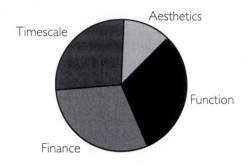

Figure 2.4 Relative weighting of failure areas

inconvenience to the Employer, despite being a financial disaster for the Contractor! The measurement of success in relation to timescale can be further complicated by issues of procurement methodology. Much can be done by an Employer and design team to mitigate design process timescale issues, by the use of alternative procurement strategies.

Finance is also becoming more subtle. The metrics are hard, and the objectives quantifiable and measurable. Nevertheless, failure in terms of finance can cover a range of potential issues:

a   cost budget inappropriate;
b   capital cost of project outside parameters;
c   whole life cost of development outside parameters;
d   cash flow at variance with planning;
e   inappropriate consideration of taxation, grant aid and subsidies.

In common with timescale it can be seen that financial issues attract different levels of criticality for different organisations. What is important to the particular Employer is the critical issue, regardless of text book norms.

Function and aesthetics are both elements of quality. The criticality is in the eye of the beholder; the comparison between chairman's door handle and the workplace ergonomics is clear. Informal conversations with, for example, production workers and office-based management within a facility will produce little common ground, apart possibly from the inadequacies of the car parking facility! Yet each opinion is equally valid and the assessment of criticality in terms of function and aesthetics demands significant input to ensure that the valid and critical issues of all stakeholders are appropriately addressed.

Scale of the problem

Numerous studies have been completed to assess the failure levels of hard measures, such as time and cost. Bromilo in 1974 (Walker 1989, p. 71), found contracts overran costs by 5 per cent on average, but only 53 per cent of all projects were completed on programme. He also noted that 41 per cent of all variations were Client generated. By implication, one might conclude that 59 per cent were generated by third parties, possibly Consultants and Contractors, but unfortunately Bromilo's studies do not confirm this. It does raise a question however.

Wood (Walker 1989, p. 72) carrying out studies in the UK in 1975, found that 40 per cent of projects had cost variances greater than 5 per cent. Average time overrun was 17 per cent, with 60 per cent of projects overrun by 5 per cent, and with 30 per cent overrunning by 20 per cent. In 1978 Graves noted 11 per cent of customers dissatisfied with the final cost of construction and 17 per cent dissatisfied with the time from design to completion.

The author's 1998 study contains some depressing statistics. It quantifies the levels of failure to which Egan alludes. Despite the Construction Industry Board survey, however, noting that marked improvements have been achieved in the last 5 years of the twentieth century, it has been found that, certainly in 1998, failure levels have not significantly changed since the studies carried out some 20 years earlier by Bromilo, Wood and Graves.

For purposes of comparison with earlier studies, it should be noted that typically Employers are quoting in excess of 10 per cent of projects failing to meet expectations and indeed a significant number are noting failure rates in excess of 35 per cent.

Taking the four briefs described previously (functional, financial, timescale and aesthetics) Figures 2.5 to 2.9 note the percentage of projects that failed fully to realise expectations.

The charts divide Employers into three distinct groups, namely:

- User Employers, which covers those undertaking projects for their own use, such as commercial business and retailers;

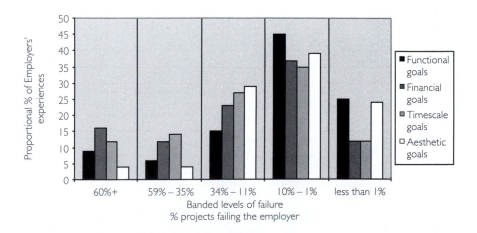

Figure 2.5 Percentage of projects failing to realise client expectation – all employers

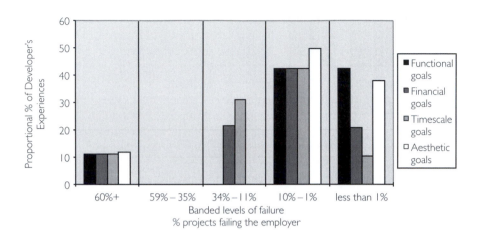

Figure 2.6 Percentage of projects failing to realise client expectation – Developer's view

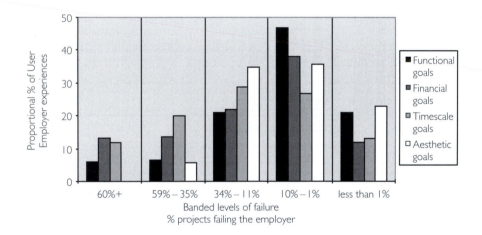

Figure 2.7 Percentage of projects failing to realise client expectation – User Employer view

- Developers undertaking projects on behalf of another party and producing projects for lease or sale, but not for their own use;
- Design and Build contractors, who are often Employers in their own right in terms of procuring design services from Consultants or other Contractors.

A consistent return between Employers as a total body (Figure 2.5) and Consultants (Figure 2.9) can be observed. The response from Design and Build Contractors as Employers, however, deviates from the general pattern of an

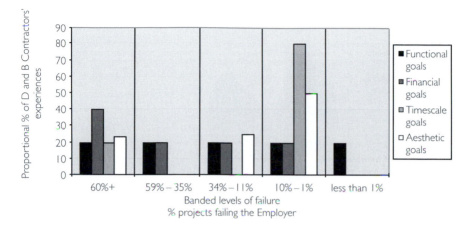

Figure 2.8 Percentage of projects failing to realise client expectation – D and B Contractor view

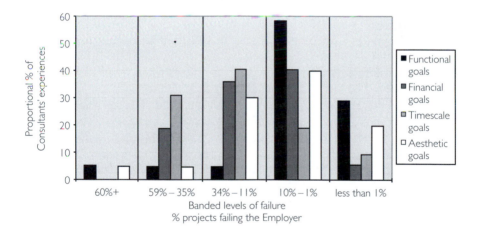

Figure 2.9 Percentage of projects failing to realise client expectation – Consultant's view

approximate normal distribution (see Figure 2.8) and reasons for this are discussed in Chapter 5.

The greatest consensus of opinion shows that two bands, 1–10 per cent and 11–34 per cent represent the level of failure experienced by the majority. The profile of Consultants matches User Employers the most closely. There is some encouragement that, despite possible gaps in perception, there is at least some level of consensus on the proportion of projects failing. As will be seen in Chapter 5 however, there is less consensus regarding the causation.

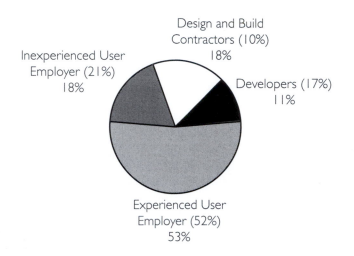

Figure 2.10 Sources of failure levels over 35 per cent in one or more briefs (Bracketed figures are percentages of survey population)

Looking at the exceptional results, namely, those indicating that 60 per cent of projects failed to meet expectations, it can be seen that Developers and Design and Build contractors are most significant. Analysis of this 'anomaly' is included in Chapter 5. Motives, goals and roles are the key to this issue. By way of comparison between Employer types, it is worthy of note that the response from User types indicating a 60 per cent+ level of failure is limited to 6 per cent under function, with 14 per cent and 12 per cent under finance and timescale respectively.

Taking an arbitrary failure rate of 35 per cent+ as being significant and 'high', Figure 2.10 clarifies the Employer type experiencing this level of failure in one or more of the four briefs. Percentages in brackets refer to the proportion of the Employer type as part of the survey population. The importance of the figures in Figure 2.10 will be discussed further in later Chapters. As a foundation the reader is encouraged to consider the percentage of failures attributable to user type in relation to the proportion that the particular user type forms, of the total Employer population.

These statistics are reinforced by regular press articles on the problems associated with procurement within the building industry. Clearly no real improvement over the last 25 years is evident. The explosion of UK litigation in respect of designers as well as contractors similarly indicates a trend which may relate to higher Client expectations, easier litigation or worsening supplier standards.

The failure levels presented in this section are laid bare and are deliberately without interpretation. It is proposed that a continued structured review of impinging issues is concluded before causation and improvement strategy is considered. Hard figures demonstrate that the scale of performance gaps within the industry is certainly worth close attention; it must surely be the aim of every Employer and every Consultant to reduce failures not just to 5 per cent, but to zero. Indeed, is not the aim of every 'Partnership' to exceed mere satisfaction and bring some delight to the table? Chapter 5 analyses these results in context of respondent type, and describes the generic reasons for failure and why they occur.

It has been shown that a performance gap is 'perceived' to exist and that failure levels are significant. This perception of failure clearly exposes a gap between expectation and realisation. It is at this point that the concept of quality, in respect of adequacy, must be considered. The following section seeks to expand the breadth of quality concepts in relation to a performance gap and the design process.

Quality

Definitions

The consideration of expectation requires an agreed definition of 'quality'. The increasing profile of quality has seen an explosion of texts on the subject, offering a variety of definitions appropriate to their context.

'Quality consists of the capacity to satisfy wants' (Edwards 1968, p. 37) provides a broad definition but obviously further requires the definition of 'wants'.

A more concise definition that brings in the concept of appropriateness and relativity is 'Quality is fitness for use' (Juran 1974, p. 2/2). The idea that quality is not absolute but something to balance against other issues is described by Broh (1982, p. 3), who notes: 'Quality is the degree of excellence at an acceptable price and the control of variability at an acceptable cost'.

Definitions proposed by Lehtinen and Lehtinen 1991 and Garvin 1988 relate to operating characteristics, reliability, conformance, service and ability to perceive quality (Usmani and Winch 1993, p. 16). This approach recognises that service and perception have a standing equal to conformance.

As part of attempts to consider Architects in the integrated supply chain, the Tavistock Institute (1999) has, in draft documentation, offered definitions and measurements of design quality. Design quality has been considered as 'the ability to delight' and design is seen as the 'value added' to a project.

Design quality is equally difficult to measure. The following headings are proposed by the Tavistock Institute (1999):

- architectural merit;
- internal quality – suitability for purpose and future adaptability;
- accessibility – championing access;
- cost in use – ease of maintenance;
- environmental friendliness and energy efficiency;
- viability of the proposed procurement route – programme methods and materials;
- overall value for money;
- cost provision and risk assessment;
- involvement of artists and tradesmen.

The metrics are altogether somewhat more elusive.

Measurement

Despite the continued investment in quality and the emergence of various techniques (Statistical Quality Control, Reliability Engineering, Zero Defects and Quality Assurance) quality remained reactive, until emergence of strategic quality management in the 1980s, which Garvin (1988, p. 20) claims has significant benefits to user satisfaction over time.

Documents such as *Defect avoidance manual – new build* (HAPM 1991) and NHBC manuals attempt to regulate design and physical quality by prescriptive methods. Similarly, codes of practice and ISO standards adopt the same approach, whereas 'quality' demands interpretation and understanding between two parties.

The subjective basis of aesthetics means that much has been written about the relevance of the built environment to art and even more about relative merits. Usmani and Winch (1993, p. 19) define aesthetic quality under the headings unity, expressiveness, magnitude, function and stability, as a means of providing a structured approach to assessment. With painful (for designers) accuracy Hill (1998, p. 3) observes that most architects imagine their work unoccupied! Allinson (1997, p. 13) however believes that aesthetics can have commodity value. Indeed, any situation where a premium is paid for the achievement of a particular appearance demonstrates this; it is an accepted part of 'branding' for many organisations, of which those in the retail and leisure industries are good examples.

Quality assurance (QA) is now commonplace within Consultancies and many Employers but, being limited to consistency, fails to address true quality. It remains, however, the key 'quality' measure applied by Government and other public sector bodies, although it fails to deal with 'people issues' (Barrett 1995b, p. 7). In the private sector where the rules are less prescriptive, Barrett (1995b, p. 4) has shown that QA is not a predominant feature in Consultant selection by Clients, and is not seen as impacting upon service quality.

Garvin's definition of quality refers to the ability to perceive service quality. Gronroos' widely published diagram (Figure 2.11) (Barrett 1993, p. 50) indicates the relevance of technical and functional quality together. How the service was rendered is equally important to what service was rendered. Richardson (1996, p. 16) and others concur that it is possible for a Client to be satisfied with technical and design input but dissatisfied with the level of service.

Total quality management (TQM) considers service provision at a higher level by addressing some of the quality 'gaps', but can fail to connect adequately with the issues of communication and understanding. The 'supple systems' approach of Barrett (1995b, p. 9) sets out to unite and create a synergy from steady state QA systems and the global, dynamic approach of TQM. Richardson (1998, p. 48) observes a move from 'reductionism' to 'holism', and sees a polarisation between 'rubberstamp QA organisations' and the proactive, service orientated (Richardson, *Architects Journal*, 5 March 1998, p. 48). Traditional QA remains a straightjacket to any organisation seeking innovation and knowledge-based growth.

It has been suggested 'tongue in cheek' that if a job goes perfectly, then the role of the Consultant may have been invisible, and where a problem in reality does occur, and a Consultant is seen to correct it, then he may gain credibility! It is

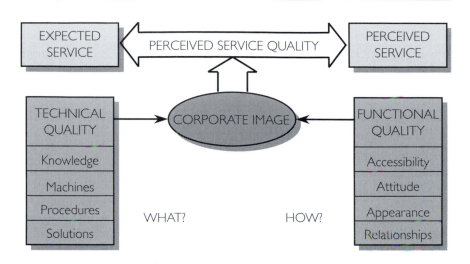

Figure 2.11 Technical and functional quality
Source: Barrett 1993, p. 50.

not a strategy to be recommended, but why should Consultants and Employers not proudly advertise success and innovation?

At the time of writing this book, the Construction Industry Council is proposing to produce key performance indicators for design (*Building*, 27 February 2000, p. 10); the relevance of these is discussed in Chapter 7. Agreement of a universally accepted measure for design is however likely to be a protracted process.

In summary, it can be said that quality is appropriateness, conditioning, relevance, fitness and so on. The assessment of what is appropriate quality is, essentially, assessment of value and fitness for purpose. Employers and Consultants should note, however, that experience and preconceptions can frequently cloud such judgements. At one extreme, an inexperienced User Employer may not be aware of what products, level of design and innovation may exist or be possible. At the other extreme, the preconception of a Consultant may impose a level of quality upon an Employer that was certainly relevant to previous projects, but represents a significant over-design in respect of the current Employer's culture, needs and resources.

The range of approaches to the definition of 'quality' are shown in Figure 2.12. The question of 'hope value' in relation to wish lists is referred to in later chapters, but it certainly should not form any part of any objective debate regarding the appropriate level of quality required.

Inevitably if the issues of quality are not addressed within the team at the outset, there is a great opportunity to fail to realise expectations by falling outside of the quality tolerance at either end of the spectrum. Even with the most willing of contributors, the divergence, typified by Figure 2.13, is inevitable if the definition of quality does not approach a level of relevant 'best' practice.

The concept of quality, in terms of appropriateness, may be applied to each of the failure areas of function, finance, timescale and aesthetics. The apparently simple act of agreement and mutual understanding of such concepts should not

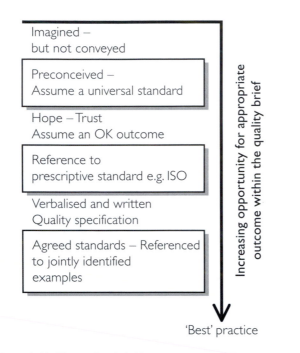

'Best' practice

Figure 2.12 The quality definition spectrum

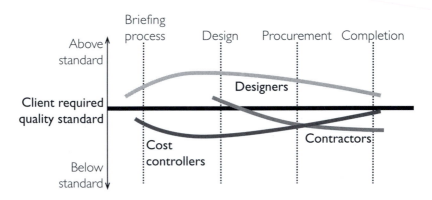

Figure 2.13 Quality drift

be assumed as an inevitable outcome of good intentions. The process of defining and agreeing a common set of quality criteria between Employer and Consultant is often considered subordinate to hard edge issues within the physical brief.

It is at this point that the project brief must be considered. The process of briefing is the single means to facilitate mutual agreement and understanding. In the broadest sense, a project needs, as part of the supply/demand spectrum of all stakeholders, the establishment of a common perception of appropriate quality, as an integral part of the briefing process. The next chapter considers current responses to briefing and reviews practice, as seen in the 1998 study.

3   The process of briefing

Current responses

Introduction

As previously stated this book is not about briefing as such. Many publications on this subject exist. Clearly briefing is the interface of almost any exchange of requirements. The description the customer gives at a delicatessen, for example, what variety of cheese and how much, is essentially a brief. The brief may be presented in many ways. The customer may specify the cheese in terms of age and source, but should he describe the quantity in terms of number of mouths to be fed, the weight or the cost? Indeed, if the customer is not able to speak the same language as the delicatessen then the use of symbolic gestures of the hands may denote the brief. Undoubtedly it would be generally agreed that construction projects demand a greater degree of sophistication, but effectively with not dissimilar limits and constraints.

The transition from Client requirement to completed project within the UK traditionally follows a linear briefing or development route. The RIBA work plan is a typical example of the process that has been adopted, not only by Architects but by the construction industry generally. Views vary widely. The traditional RIBA plan of work is broadly supported by some (Salisbury 1998, p. 58) who suggest that work that is restricted to single stages of the plan and is compartmentalised can be more effective. Conversely, others (Barrett 1995a, p. 77) believe that this process is inappropriate and propose a cyclical briefing process. The four parties normally involved in the building process (designers, paying clients, regulators and constructor) have, traditionally, restricted communication with end users and other stakeholders, despite the observed benefits of such communication (Barrett 1995a, p. 87).

Prime contracting and other partnership initiatives endeavour to address this issue, but mere involvement of all those involved does not ensure success. Health Trusts have been good examples for many years of the Employer who involves a full range of representatives throughout the briefing and design development process. Success, however, is dependent upon internal Employer management preventing the mushrooming of 'Empires'. The 'buying in' of all involved needs to be uniform. A common protocol and understanding is essential, to avoid the negative energies of the 'silent majority'.

Lack of time is commonly given in response to concerns of inadequacies in briefing and restricted communication. Egan refers to this issue and calls for greater resources to be allocated to the briefing process and more appropriate methods to be employed for briefing and involvement; unfortunately this is nothing new. Earlier works, such as the RICS study, research by Higgins and Jessop in 1965, and Goodacre in 1980, all showed that insufficient time and resource was given to the briefing process. Thirty-five years later the same calls are being heard.

Somogyi's 1999 study noted that the three most common reasons for contract failures were:

1   inadequate information;
2   late information;
3   inadequate design brief.

The study considered projects as a whole, including the built form, and for this reason it makes 'inadequate design brief' so much more critical as an event in the context of the overall procurement process.

It is commendable that the profile of briefing and the need for communication is high on the agenda of debate. It is disappointing, however, that except for some notable examples, current systems of project inception, briefing and communication remain static. It is therefore not surprising that levels of dissatisfaction remain high.

It is therefore essential to consider the brief, and briefing process, as an integral part of any investigation into the interfaces between Employers and their design teams. The following section considers briefing in the general sense, providing a perspective on existing standards, guidance and studies. The second part of this chapter considers the reality of briefing in 1998, as shown by the author's study. Chapter 6 continues to consider in depth current practice, and Chapter 7 explores the alternatives purporting to be 'Egan in practice'.

Briefing

Definitions

Most literature and research in the field of expectation and realisation refer to the necessity for a good brief. Definitions of the 'brief' have a high degree of similarity but include some subtle nuances. Salisbury (1998, p. 1) notes: 'It is more than a verbal exchange of ideas. It is a creative act which shapes the subsequent building.' Other definitions include: 'a communicable statement of intent' (Sanoff 1977) and 'a statement of an architectural problem' (Preiser 1993). However, these definitions imply a document or similar fixed product, and a broader definition needs to be sought.

Describing 'programming', as briefing is known in the USA, Murray, Gameson and Hudson (Preiser 1993, p. 431) note that it is 'the communication process between a Client organisation and the construction professionals to produce a statement from which a facility which satisfies the Clients requirements can be produced'. Their definition still refers to a statement but places an emphasis upon the process.

The Construction Industry Board (1997) guide, written for Employers and potential Employers, follows this theme, noting: 'Briefing is the process by which a Client informs others of his or her needs, aspirations and desires, either formally or informally, and a brief is a formal document which sets out a Client's requirements in detail'.

Barrett's definition of briefing, further to the conclusion of numerous case studies, extends well beyond the concept of a singular document or act, and describes it as: 'The process running throughout the construction project by which means the Client's requirements are progressively captured and translated in to effect' (Barrett and Stanley 1999, p. 134). He notes that briefing is 'seen as a process and not an event' (Barrett and Stanley 1999, p. 3).

The role of the 'brief taker' is slightly incongruous in relation to the concept of a process, as it again suggests a singular act. Nevertheless this often reflects reality, and as a consequence, the process of briefing can be heavily influenced by the personal aspirations, skills and knowledge of the participants. The process described must involve a series of briefs developing levels of detail as it progresses, involving feedback, and predicting the quality of the project (CIB 1997, p. 5). It assumes the earliest definition of appropriate quality, as previously discussed. Unfortunately, current work practice, as embodied in the RIBA work plan for example, compartmentalises briefing and restricts it to a single early act. Gameson (Barrett and Males 1991, p. 175) and Lock (1992, p. 40) among many see it as an ongoing process that should continue until the building is complete.

Despite wide acceptance that a good brief is essential to success, many projects see the process severely under-resourced. Becker (1991, p. 123) believes that many organisations grasp solutions or concentrate on small issues, and that no other investments (other than property) would be made so blindly. Barrett and Stanley's (1999, p. 11) case studies show that there is little evidence of a rationale: it is 'messy' and 'a jumble of conflicting and confused aims'.

Lack of development in terms of a strategic brief is clearly evident and, as previously noted, designers are rarely involved even when a strategic brief is formally considered.

Nutt (1988, p. 130) notes that the risks attached to traditional briefing are attributable to:

- dependence upon linear logic;
- concentration on visible ideas;
- limited source of innovative ideas;
- lack of quantitative evaluation.

Value engineering techniques are beginning to impact upon the last deficiency, but the first three remain current.

Briefing should bring together Employers, Designers and, increasingly, Constructors to solve problems. 'Poor or inadequate brief is often behind the failure, with blame generally laid at Designer's door', according to Atkin, Clarke and Smith (1996, p. 6): 'Sometimes blame has to be shared equally with the Client for no other reason than failure to involve the Designer and other members of the project team sooner. That designers do not always succeed in achieving this earlier involvement, should be a matter of concern.'

Briefing can be a process of expansion and clarification, but it can also be used as a cage for an Employer and an excuse for both design team and Supplier/Contractors. It has been suggested (Barrett and Stanley 1999, p. 44) most strongly that there should be 'emphasis on the verb and not the noun'. As discussed in later sections, however, it is not as simple as the above might suggest. The bringing together of Employer and Consultants at an early stage will only be beneficial if the issues of motivation, common language, goals and strategy are resolved at the outset.

The briefing process should be seen as a series of interdependent briefing exercises covering a variety of agendas. Nutt (1993, p. 30), in proposing such a subdivision, notes that the:

> ... importance of the design brief has been overstated, it has dominated the process as a whole giving unrealistic expectations over the responsibilities of the designer for the subsequent use of buildings and facilities in the medium term and beyond. In contrast, the organisational briefing process remains underdeveloped and the facility programming brief has only recently begun to receive expert attention.

Spedding (1994, p. 76) endorses this view, specifically highlighting the Facilities Management brief and noting that design is successful where understanding of the initial concept has been transferred to continuing users and managers. He notes that the 'Facility Manager's role is to integrate user interests (demand) and building team (supply).' Along similar lines, McLennan (Preiser 1993, p. 338) proposes that facility planning should be the central focus of a strategic brief. Practice shows however that the facility brief rarely exists.

In short, the headlong rush to the singular solution, the physical brief and the definition of the 'deliverables', provides an quick but highly unsatisfactory project path.

Information flow

The 'traditional single stage brief' targets short-term needs. Maximum flexibility, however, for the Employer can only be assured by essential information being collected at each stage and decisions being made at the last responsible moment. This is not endorsement of the design process that frequently accompanies Design and Build. This procurement route often sees the ongoing development of the brief and design translated into a construction programme, resulting in an unprepared Client being pressured into making briefing commitments with the penalty of 'delay' being laid at their door.

The RIBA plan of work conversely encourages Clients to obtain as much information as they can early in the process; consequently the brief can become too detailed too soon, precluding innovative or creative solutions (Barrett 1995a, p. 89). It is suggested by others that this is the failing of Contractor/Quantity Surveyor type project management techniques (Atkin, Clarke and Smith 1996, p. 15). Many readers will be familiar with the demand for 'all information before we can start'; it is patently untrue and unnecessary.

Despite a level of support for the RIBA work plan, Salisbury and White (1980, p. 19) see briefing as an information flow moving from strategic to detailed Client information which must be capable of looping back for re-appraisal and adjustment. Walker (1989, p. 76) refers to this as a 'dynamic approach'.

Several sources have developed alternative models along the same lines:

- Barrett adopts the 'loop brief', offering continuous appraisal and reappraisal.
- Stichting Bouwresearch of Rotterdam propose a system following traditional phases, but minimising the amount of information required for each phase to enable it to proceed to the next phase. In this way, each phase works towards greater detail but avoids detailed issues clouding more strategic decisions (Barrett 1995a, p. 91).
- Following the ideas of Becker, Barrett and Salisbury, Gray, Hughes and Bennett (1994, p. 6) propose a 'continuous whirling process model', offering similar feedback and continuous input benefits.

The wider use of such loop feedback systems of briefing are constrained by current procurement systems. The emphasis on early fixed 'deliverables' is a response to a lack of trust in many contracting parties. Trust is an issue that is equally relevant to Consultants as it is to Contractors.

Briefing is a means to an end, where the end is the built product which is created by a flow of information, leading to a flow of materials. Usmani and Winch (1993, p. 6) use a river analogy. The structural approach of project management defines the boundaries and scopes (the banks). The technique-based approach defines management and control (dams and canals), and the 'water' itself is the information flow. It is suggested that even before feasibility studies start, a reservoir of information exists in information fields. The extraction or translation of this information, however, is a major stumbling block to the narrowing of the gap between expectation and realisation. It is an issue considered in later chapters in relation to issues of knowledge management.

It is unfortunate that there are often strict limits on the amount of time and energy devoted to information gathering by Consultants and Employers alike. Cohen (Preiser 1993, p. 454) and recently Egan both endorse this view. Risks are attached to the neglect of information gathering. Carole Brief argued, in 1977, that uncertainty is the difference between the amount of information required for the task, and the amount of information already possessed for the task; therefore reduction of uncertainty demands increased information (Usmani and Winch 1993, p. 8)

Few would disagree with this view. However a variety of sources (Barrett 1995a; Salisbury 1998) conclude that the Employer's goals are often forgotten by the end of the project. It suggested that it is lack of the strategic brief that allows

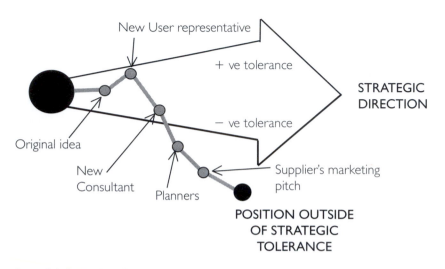

Figure 3.1 Strategic drift

this to happen. The concentration on a short-term project brief may expediently deal with the problem in hand, but following down the 'trumpet of uncertainty', overall strategy can be missed. Where all goals are 'forgotten', this really is a euphemism for 'no real long-term strategy to start with' (See Figure 3.1.)

Techniques for briefing

Numerous sources (CIB 1997, p. 9; O'Reilly 1992, p. 8) concur on the attributes of a 'good' brief, listing such worthy aims as: clarity, priority, consistency, realism, relevance, flexibility. On the basis that few facilities will remain in the same use class throughout their life, Nutt (1988, p. 133) proposes an active strategic approach to briefing, and focuses on five key issues:

- flexibility;
- contingency design;
- least commitment;
- loose fit;
- indeterminacy.

The usual expectation, however, and the reality is an initial list of accommodation and standards. Even those who advocate the traditional RIBA route agree that this is not the best way to begin briefing and suggest the examination of present circumstance and future requirements (Barrett 1995, p. 2).

Another common technique of briefing is a checklist. Research (Preiser 1993, p. 432) into communication within the briefing process, by Higgins and Jessop in 1963, Mackinder and Marvin in 1982 and O'Reilly in 1987, all refer to checklists predominating, together with questionnaires and meetings. This can place a very heavy burden upon the Employer/Customer (Lock 1992, p. 49) who may be expected to sign off requirements that are based on closed questions from a predetermined list. As Murray and Gameson and Hudson note, checklists can have both positive and negative attributes (Preiser 1993, p. 435), preventing oversights, but promoting preconception and inhibition. In reality, the usefulness of checklists is limited to simple repeat projects where there is a clear long-term repetitive understanding between Employer and Consultants and, most importantly, a steady state demand. Innovative use can assist with the identification of risk, particularly in relation to finance, time life span (O'Reilly 1992, pp. 14–27), but care is required if they are not to become straightjackets.

Other common techniques include:

1   questionnaires from design team to client, which are in effect active and organic checklists (Salisbury and White 1980, p. 84);
2   'briefing conferences' and 'design sessions' which can be effective, but also run the risk of 'instant architecture' (O'Reilly 1992, p. 17), generally favouring the most vocal;
3   performance specifications: their intermittent use would appear to have both supporters and critics. Harrison and Keeble (1983, p. 44) consider performance specifications reduce the scope for technical arguments about quality. Others suggest that they simply highlight problems regarding the liability for the overall performance (Lupton and Stellakis 1995, p. 55). The evaluation of the softer issues does not appear easy with this technique.

The most appropriate strategy must be determined by the Client and the project type (Salisbury 1998, p. 184). Employers may be:

•   a first time client;
•   a regular repeat client;
•   an expert client;
•   a multi-headed corporation.

Similarly buildings may fall into different types, namely:

•   special very high quality with little reference material;
•   existing buildings with phased works;
•   multi-use buildings;
•   standard buildings with extensive guidance (Salisbury and White 1980, p. 25).

As noted previously there is no one universal best practice, but the concept of feedback, fluidity and flow are essential, and will be explored in later chapters.

Briefing – reality of practice in 1998

There has been an increasing amount of research into the issue of briefing and a correspondingly widespread dissemination of information to the construction industry. It should be of major concern therefore that in practice, briefing remains a simple mechanical exercise concentrating on physical delivery by means of datasheets and checklists, and thus frequently misses the wider strategic implications and the 'how questions'.

As part of the 1998 study outlined in Chapter 1, Employers and Consultants were questioned to ascertain how briefs were produced in practice and upon what they were based. The following section summarises the responses to set into context current 'normal' practice against 'best' practice concepts. The results are presented as raw data, with analysis being considered in later chapters, after the conclusion of this review of 'impinging issues'.

Despite the current emphasis on process as opposed to the singular act, briefing in practice is an event that happens quickly and results in a fixed document. The perception of both Employers and Consultants is generally that of a tangible volume which could receive the 'QA stamp' before any lines are drawn. In fairness, there is evidence that the brief does grow and expand with time, but there is little evidence of review.

Four subdivisions of the briefing process were considered, based upon the three areas of concern identified previously and a fourth area, aesthetics, which could not be reasonably ignored in the context of design:

1   function;
2   finance;
3   timescale;
4   aesthetics.

A wide range of techniques are used to express Employers' requirements. The results received from Consultants and all types of Employers were consistent. Figure 3.2 shows that 'targets' are the most common form for conveying requirements, followed closely by 'verbal briefing meetings', 'wish lists' and 'prescriptive written statements'. The latter tend to be associated with more structured organisations, either public sector or highly experienced repeat Clients. Examples of the latter include retailers with multiple outlets endeavouring to achieve a degree of standardisation. Similarly, organisations such as the Ministry of Defence (MoD), until recently, expended a great deal of time producing extremely prescriptive briefs before involving third parties.

Figure 3.3 subdivides the brief and relates the use of media type to a specific elemental brief. As expected, financial and timescale briefs are generally more objectively defined using harder communications media.

'Wish lists' are most evident in association with user meetings related to function and aesthetics. Interestingly their 'status' is accepted by both Consultant and Employer, as noted by comment and interview. The fact that such items are accepted at face value makes the task no less difficult for Consultants to interpret. Is it reasonable for a designer to be given, for example, the task of choosing between gold-plated fittings or an additional bedroom if budget permits, in a private domestic situation. It is proposed that any items that are considered non-essential to a project, first, undergo an appropriate level of value engineering to

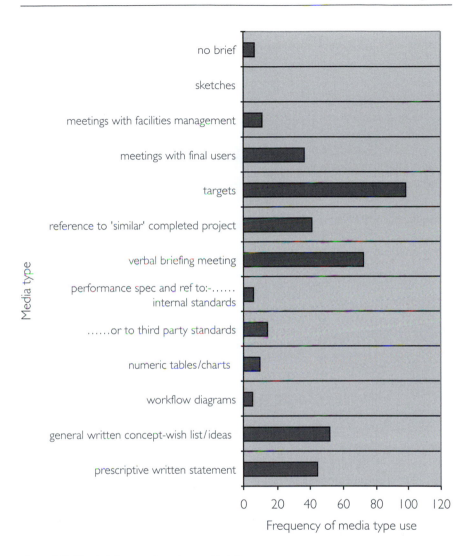

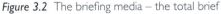

Figure 3.2 The briefing media – the total brief

determine objectively their status. Second, if the project has such a degree of uncertainty that 'wish lists' do have a place, then it is essential that they are evaluated and given sliding scale of merit. It is increasingly critical with multi-headed Clients to ensure that all members of the Client team 'buy in' to an agreed schedule of importance to those non-essential items. It does, however, appear that well managed and value-engineered projects have no place for wish lists, as they have their origin in 'hope value' derived from the competitive procurement system.

Questions related to the basis of information generation attempt to demonstrate how the ideas and requirements are conceived. Although the way in which

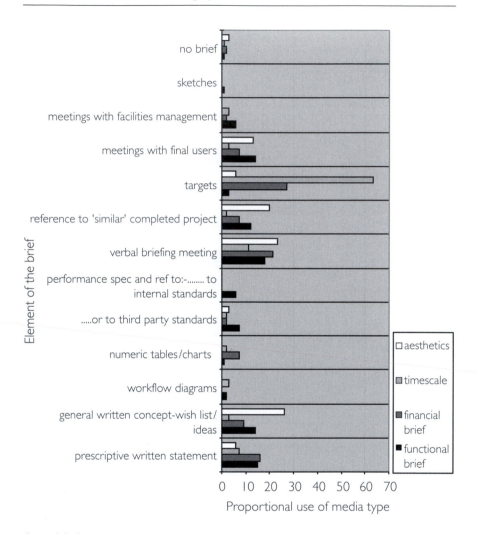

Figure 3.3 The use of alternative briefing media

a brief is presented may have an influence on the effectiveness of translation or interpretation, it is the basis of the brief that must be fundamental to the success of achieving and satisfying needs. As Figure 3.4 indicates, Employers note that 'experience' is the primary basis for brief specification, whereas the Consultants *perceive* that the basis relates to harder data and refer much more to 'organisation led demand' and 'the strategic business plan'.

Chapters 5 and 6 continue the discussion to consider how this disturbing profile of briefing effects the performance gap. Interviews revealed that variations of perception between Consultant and Employer, and indeed the lack of strategic input, was greater in actual current practice than even implied by the survey responses.

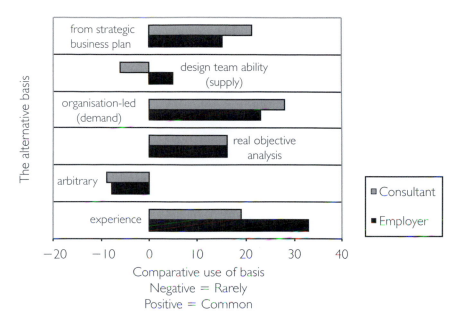

Figure 3.4 The basis of brief specification – Employers' view

It is evident from the author's 1998 survey that many of the concerns expressed in recent literature, research and guidance notes, as reviewed in the previous section, are indeed current in everyday practice. Evidence of 'best' practice or innovative briefing concepts do exist but are certainly not in common usage. In contrast to traditional stereotypes, sections of the public sector, on the back of government initiatives, are leading new working practices, while other sectors remain true to form and carry the baggage of bureaucracy and 'procedure'. The supposed bastion of innovation, the private sector, certainly does not automatically warrant this description and needs to take due regard of government initiatives, regardless of political origin.

4 Hurdles and barriers

Hurdles

An appreciation of the process, the goals and the failures is fundamental to any strategy for improvement. Equally important, however, is appreciating the hurdles that are to be overcome to enable these improvement strategies to be facilitated. It is a fact that a whole range of hurdles exist. These cannot be ignored or, in the real world, avoided. Differences in communication techniques, language and subsequent translation of the language into the design product mean that the existence of certain hurdles must be accepted. Techniques need to be developed to ensure that they become simple obstacles, as opposed to absolute barriers.

Hand in hand with the concepts of language and perception go issues of culture and skill base. Much is written about 'partnering' between organisations. Senior managers of such organisations may achieve an understanding of their respective culture and skill base and, potentially, their overall agenda, it is rare, however, that the ' working' team members have such understanding. It would seem that without a common appreciation of skills, cultures and agendas there can be no formation of a real team, no clear understanding of roles and probably little respect for any leadership structure.

Too many projects suffer from negative power exerted from within the team, either within a single organisation, whether it be Employer or Consultant, or between organisations forming the total team. It is not uncommon for issues of leadership to escalate to professional rivalry culminating in resentment, and yet again more negative power.

The hurdles that must be addressed are generically those of communication and appropriateness of team structure. These are issues that involve not just the organisations as corporate entities, but particularly the individual. This chapter also considers facility management and Users. It is not suggested that these two parties are necessarily hurdles in themselves, but rather that exclusion can provide the seeds of subsequent failure and dissatisfaction. Simple *inclusion* within a team, however, does not automatically ensure success and it is necessary to ensure that the issues of roles, culture and communication are again fully addressed in order that input from facility management and Users is positively utilised.

Communication

Any situation involving one or more persons working together for a single objective demands understanding of those shared goals and a common form of communication. The starting point of the briefing process depends upon the knowledge base of each party. Assessing the level at which to start is critical (Gray et al. 1994, p. 4).

The element of 'trust' is a powerful element in successful communication, and has been identified in many studies (CIB 1997, p. 9; Preiser 1993, p. 432). It is equally critical for Consultants to understand the Employer's initial motivation to invest time and money in design (Cuff 1996, p. 103). It is also important for Employers to understand the Consultant's motive. The interpretation of 'partnering' by some into 'free feasibilities for the same low fees' is simply not acceptable. The complaint of 'insufficient' design development raised by many Employers is an inevitable consequence.

The simple act of communication is often taken for granted. Carole Driver (RIBA 1995, p. 103) refers to 'tuning in to clients' and the 'Active listening Architect'. She notes that 'they don't understand or try to fit in with client organisations.... Hearing happens automatically, listening is a more active skill'. It is a two-way exercise, of course: Employers need to listen without the cloud of preconception. All parties need to question in a 'no blame' environment to ensure a real understanding. 'Tuning in' means understanding the meaning behind the words, not just the words themselves.

Peters (1987, p. 73) notes that many innovative companies get their best ideas from customers. The concept of listening and constantly reviewing performance with Clients is a consistent thread in the achievement of quality. Yet within the construction industry the most basic of reviews is unusual. For example, the post-occupancy evaluation, even in the form of a telephone enquiry on the completion of a project, remains a rare occurrence.

Language and perception

Communication skills include verbal and non-verbal media. Research by the British Institute of Management into the importance of non-verbal communication shows that 10 per cent of a message is conveyed by intonation/expression, and 40 per cent by body language (Pennington 1986, p. 171).

Beattie (Pennington 1986, p. 171) studied speaker switches involving interruption, and Gameson collected data and produced interaction of profiles, using Bales categories. Results show that experienced Employers dominate meetings, whereas with naive Employers, the Consultant dominates. Although this finding is not 'earth shattering', it sets an agenda for a potential gap in expectation, as real requirements or advice are buried beneath a mound of emphatic and opinionated preconception.

Psychology based research relates perception to language at a global level (Davenport 1994, p. 156). Benjamin Lee Whorf and Edward Sapir produced the

'Sapir-Whorf' linguistic relativity hypothesis. Studies showed that culture, language and perception interrelate to the extent that if you cannot describe the difference between two things you probably cannot perceive any difference. At the strong end of the hypothesis, you cannot perceive what you cannot describe; at the more realistic end of the hypothesis, the language we use influences the way we regard things.

Various other studies by Burnstein, Shipman and Burr (Gross 1996, p. 323), and Vygotsky show that there is a relationship between the elaboration of language and social background/culture. At a practice based level, Gameson (Barrett and Males 1991, p. 168) notes that language differs between various professionals, together with their traditional social and educational backgrounds. The potential for misunderstanding between individuals is great.

At a theoretical level, concepts like 'privacy' and 'crowding' cannot be interpreted accurately in the same way as physical definitions such as 'the kitchen' (Preiser 1993, p. 412). As a response Winer (Pennington 1986, p. 172) proposes that, at any meeting, three elements are necessary, if understanding is to be achieved:

1   encoder;
2   code;
3   decoder.

The practical achievement of these three elements, however, requires, first, the parties to realise that there is in fact a language difference and, second, a set of 'translation rules' to be developed. As Professor Randolph Quirk noted (Richardson 1996, p. 60): 'Every particular use of English is to some extent reflected in, and determines the form of the language that is used for that particular purpose'.

Translation

A key issue is the translation of the Employer's requirements, which may be subjective, prescriptive and conflicting as the basis for design work (Lupton and Stellakis 1995, p. 49). Bertrand notes that the gap exists between programming (briefing, in the UK) and design because the criteria do not readily translate into a 3D model (Preiser 1993, p. 410).

Robinson and Weeks proposed that analysis, synthesis, verbal and graphic media should be integral. Drawings are a means to an end (Salisbury 1998, p. 137), but it is acknowledged that there is an art to reading them, and 3D visualisation from 2D graphics can be problematic. Alternative three-dimensional perspectives and models are noted as expensive and potentially misleading, as they freeze a design. The understanding of 'design development' needs to be appreciated by Employers and Consultants alike. Sketch schemes and budgets so often become tablets of stone and hard constraints on the future advancement of design.

The classic paper trail of design development in terms of scribbled sketches and ideas, developing over time to conventional drawings, may be acceptable for designers, but is not so helpful to most Employers. Key visual drawings, montages and mock-ups are much more relevant. Models can also be used unscrupulously as a persuasive and influential medium. However, *appropriate* models and virtual reality are considered to be highly relevant and the cost of their production can be repaid many times over if it ensures that the project meets Employers' aspirations. The old Chinese proverb seems quite appropriate: '100 tellings is not as good as one seeing'.

Simple decisions regarding communication and visualisation techniques can be far-reaching. For example, many drawings are produced on CAD (computer-aided design) stations with a variety of multi-coloured lines which the CAD operator has no difficulty in reading. Most commonly, however, the output is black and white and the spider web drawing that eventually results is incomprehensible to the Employer, who may have little experience of reading drawings.

The use of montages and photographs of existing work from a range of designers has been proven to be a very efficient way of clarifying the values and aspirations of any particular Employer. It satisfies the demands of an Employer wishing to make fast progress and satisfies the Consultant by avoiding countless abortive computer models and sketches.

Figure 4.1 shows a range of techniques, each of which are excellent in their own right and appropriate in particular circumstances. With demands on 'fast-track' and efficient development of the design process, it can be seen that a mix involving 'the montage', 'the composite' and the 3D CAD model has much to recommend it.

The design leader is responsible for ensuring that the Client fully understands the proposals and is able to agree that they meet their objectives – it is rarely satisfactory for Clients to be shown Designers' conceptual sketches alone, and still less outline plans of rooms (Garvin 1988, p. 25). Regardless of the medium it is essential that all involved acknowledge both the purpose and the stage of development. The 'Constable' painting shown on the wall of the early internal perspective may only be indicative!

Information technology and systems

The previous example of the CAD screen compared to output shows the disadvantages that inappropriate IT can have. However, the positive benefits are potentially boundless, but to a large extent remain untapped in the construction world. With the exception of CAD and low-level applications such as spreadsheets and word processing, IT has yet to make significant in-roads into the construction and procurement process.

The study by Atkin, Clarke and Smith investigates IT use in Client and Designer led organisations. It shows that there is some use of IT at briefing and design stages, but concludes much more emphasis needs to be placed on the early stages when Clients' needs are articulated into, and interpreted into, a working design solution. It is believed that the stage of translating business needs into a workable design, in particular, can be assisted by IT systems (Atkin, Clarke and Smith 1996, p. 1). The benefits of IT systems at briefing are defined as:

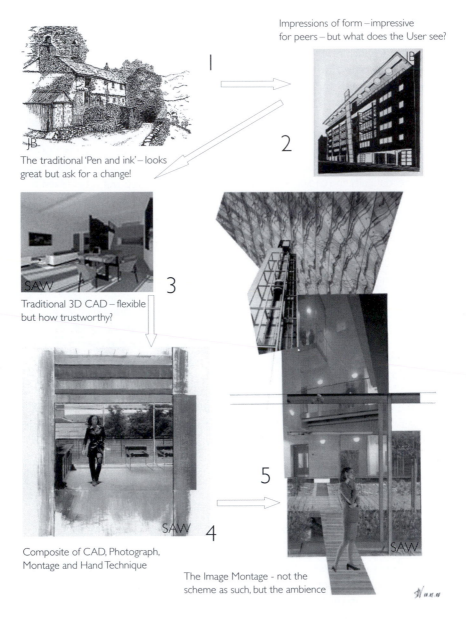

Impressions of form – impressive
for peers – but what does the User see?

1

2

The traditional 'Pen and ink' – looks
great but ask for a change!

Traditional 3D CAD – flexible
but how trustworthy?

3

5

4

Composite of CAD, Photograph,
Montage and Hand Technique

The Image Montage - not the
scheme as such, but the ambience

Figure 4.1 Range of graphical techniques

- control of design information;
- better distribution of information;
- quicker turn-around of information;
- risk management, quality of information;
- cost reduction;
- increased efficiency and competitive edge (Atkin, Clarke and Smith 1996, p. 30).

Current innovative use of web-based project hubs is demonstrating that these advantages are tangible and available now. The research by the University of Reading provides an international perspective on Client 'unhappiness' and attempts to deal with communication by means of IT systems using an improved checklist concept (Preiser 1993, p. 428).

The key strengths of IT systems are only recently becoming appreciated. The issues of knowledge management and the spread of information, referred to previously, are fundamental to the concept of providing an appropriate brief. Later chapters explore in greater depth the existence of knowledge hubs and how they can be applied to the design process. The composite value of layers of brief, namely strategic, tactical and operational, can only be extracted by use of an integrated system, which allows the production of briefs under a range of headings: for example, the facility brief, the time brief, the quality brief. More sophisticated use of IT systems would appear to have great potential in managing this complex set of demands.

A current DETR (1998–99) sponsored research programme into the use of IT in the design and construction industries is already observing low levels of use. Organisations using IT as a graphic medium are becoming centres of excellence at the expense of other organisations which retain traditional presentation and management techniques. It is not all sweetness and light however. The graphics produced by IT packages have the potential to mislead as well as to inform. Beyond the problems of inadequate construction output quality, there are issues of 'adjustment'. The 'artists' impression' was initially made redundant by prescriptive and realistic CAD imagery, but IT now offers more tricks than the artist's brush ever did. The appearance of accuracy means that IT can be a dangerous tool in the wrong hands. A recently publicised planning appeal procedure involving aerial photographs, produced by both sides, demonstrated the point: identical but different! – 'the case of the vanishing building'.

Agendas

There appears to be a consensus of opinion that a variety of agendas will occur within any team.

The definition of the 'multi-headed' Client supports the existence of multiple agendas within the Employer, which can be repeated throughout all the contributors. Richardson suggests that 'all prospective Clients have a hidden agenda'; there may be a series of issues that they require to be addressed, but they are unable to articulate them in a way that can be translated into a building (Richardson 1996, p. 60). It is often seen that building works can be a mechanism for instigating an aspect of change management or process. The more cynical reader may suggest that Employers and Consultants may both have 'hidden agendas', but they are often deliberately concealed. The lack of trust that develops from this belief continues to plague the industry; it is to the detriment of both Employers and Consultants, all of whom spend time re-working, checking and procrastinating, as they attempt to ensure that the other parties are acting honourably.

Two parallel surveys covering Employers and Consultants are reviewed by

Touche Ross (RIBA 1993, p. 7). A number of key themes are identified, noting that Architects, for example, and their Clients approached a project with different aspirations and priorities. The divergent set of interests of Consultants, as identified by the RIBA, can be summarised:

immediate revenue generation;
continued revenue generation;
personal needs – opinion of peers and public;
minimal use of resources.

Employers seek, not unreasonably, potentially conflicting requirements summarised by:

value for money;
maximum (devoted) resources;
adherence to their own requirements;
maximum design development and ongoing value engineering.

Contrary to discourse on issues of value, it has been suggested that Designers simply contemplate the art object and not the occupation. Architecture has been seen as 'a physical phenomenon with specific materials and dimension ... unoccupied' (Hill 1998, p. 5). It has recently been suggested that 'cultural and social codes reinforce art over the everyday' (Hill 1998, p. 5).
      This view is as extreme as the call for faceless functional utilitarian living in workplace cubes. It demonstrates the extremes of view that can exist at the beginning of the twenty-first century between various factions of the same industry. Progress can only be made by the acceptance of the correctness of both views. Strategies need to be developed to enable both to co-exist within a single project, to create delight and utility simultaneously.
      The acceptance of the different agendas and systems of reconciliation would appear to be fundamental to the development of true 'partnerships'. But cost remains a major issue. A survey regarding fees (Garvin 1988, p. 43) by the Association of Consulting Engineers demonstrated that competitive fees had given rise to:

1   significantly less consideration of design alternatives;
2   less checking;
3   general quality being minimised.

A total of 20 indicators determined that reduced fees have a detrimental effect. This is rarely overtly discussed but is implied by several sources (Preiser 1993, p. 432) relating to timescales and quality. The government's compulsory competitive tendering rules and the Latham proposals (30 per cent reduction in construction costs, to which professional fees contribute 12–20 per cent) are driving the commercial agenda. Low wages and little standardisation mean that the UK has the lowest input costs into construction but the highest output cost, within

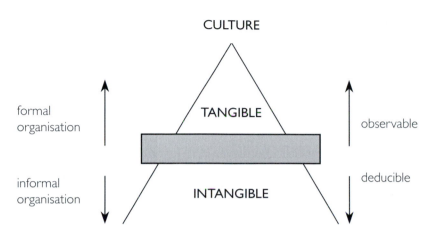

Figure 4.2 The context of 'culture'

Europe (Office of Science and Technology 1995, p. 9). This is considered to be a disincentive to innovation, but maintains the commercial agenda at a high profile.

Egan refers to the above issues, proposing less dependence upon competitive price tendering, increased profit levels and increased standardisation. Changes in EC directives during the year 2000 are giving the public sector, at least, the ability to move away from compulsive competitive tendering. The often stated objective of assessing quality *and* cost is commendable but fraught with difficulties. The process of procuring Consultant services often means that even when quality criteria can be defined, there remains little difference between the Consultants, other than the highly visible cost element. Consultants scoring similarly on quality issues but differing on cost generally means only one of two things: either the profit element is higher or the resourcing is less or of a lower calibre. Employers should seek resource time budgets against which they assess cost, if they have any aspirations to improving levels of Consultant input. It is not unreasonable for profit levels to be declared by Consultant *and* Employer. The potential reconciliation of such agendas is proposed by a series of 'Prime Contracting' and 'Partnership' arrangements discussed in Chapter 7.

Culture

Culture concerns the level of importance attached to particular issues (Kernohan *et al.* 1996, p. 17). Mutual understanding is required between members, of project goals, at a level beyond the purely physical. Culture comprises a composite of visible and inherent qualities and values, modified by sets of formal and informal 'rules' (see Figure 4.2).

Projects require the bringing together of different parties, both internal and external, into the 'team'. Barrett (1995a, p. 86) observes that Clients who choose a team at odds with their own world view run the risk of being swept away, but also notes the importance of developing systems that allow different learning and working styles (Kolb's learning cycle (Barrett and Males 1991, p. 137)) to cohabit within the team. A compatibility of cultural webs appears essential. Too often the level of compatibility or incompatibility is not established until the project is well underway and invariably struggling.

Becker (1991, p. 61) accepts that in the past design teams often had inadequate briefs with no reference to the organisation, and believes that the facility manager has a pivotal role in understanding the traditional Consultant's culture, roles and the anticipated deliverables.

Mutual visits to Employers' and Consultants' offices, as well as other projects, are suggested by Salisbury and White (1980, p. 15). This may appear basic advice, but such visits rarely occur in any meaningful or structured way. 'Lunches' and other corporate activities may well be a very successful way of understanding small groups of individuals, but do little to understand the total company culture or ambience. Organisations frequently come together on the basis of contact between Principals or Directors and find shortly after that teams of individuals are attempting to work together with little understanding of their respective structures, cultures and motivations. It is again briefing, but in this respect briefing within the organisation, both Employer and Consultant.

The Author's study reinforces this view. The lack of a service brief between Consultant and Employer is frequently cited as a reason for failure. Later chapters consider this issue in greater depth, together with strategies for developing an appropriate service brief.

The players

The multi-headed employer

As early as 1966 the Tavistock Institute (Walker 1989, p. 60) was noting that Employers were a complex system of differing interests, and that the relationship is seldom with a single member of the building industry. Competing sets of objectives, values and understandings have resulted in much aborted work.

The multi-headed Employer, where there are differences between Controllers, Payees and Users, is found in both the public and private sector. Although such multiplicity is more common in the public sector (Preiser 1993, p. 362), Walker and Hughes describe one private sector Employer consisting of 40 different management units, of which 30 had the power to make recommendations (Walker 1989, p. 82).

Complete understanding of the Employer's organisation is rare; frequently, some members of the Consultant team do not meet 'the Client', and the project team leader often acts as a surrogate client. The potential cultural differences that may exist between team members of a Consultant and Employer body, that previously have not even met are obvious. The need for understanding throughout a team is fundamental.

Good practice recommends that large Client bodies should appoint a single active liaison person who should not be simply a 'post box' (O'Reilly 1992, p. 6). This practice has worked well, but depends upon the quality of the person appointed and, importantly, the level of authority that they carry (Usmani and Winch 1993, P. 9). The task is critical in any organisation that has a series of potentially conflicting demands and 'contributors'. It is essentially the role of 'management' but with the added need to convey a single message to an outside party, namely the Consultant. The same arguments could equally be applied to the 'multi-headed Consultant'. Employers and Consultants alike have cited the failure to appoint an appropriate person for 'liaison' as being a key element in project failures.

Despite the wealth of statistics regarding the construction industry there appears to be no consensus about the nature of 'the Employer'. Employer types are defined by Gameson (Barrett and Males 1991, p. 165) by dependence upon their frequency of procurement. At one extreme, the HMSO 1989 Professional Liability Study (Gray et al. 1994, p. 2) claims that the 'Experienced Employer' now accounts for over 75 per cent of project clients; at the other extreme, Atkin, Clarke and Smith (1996, p. 14) note that most Employers are inexpert, have no contact with the construction industry and are essentially 'naïve'.

The Author's 1998 study defines Employers in a similar manner and finds 71 per cent of respondents to be 'experienced'. This is a clear correlation with the HMSO study. Chapter 5 describes the population of the study in greater detail. The fact that a high proportion of Employers have regular construction demands, or indeed are property professionals in their own right, has a significant implication for Consultants attempting to close the performance gap.

Employers cannot be simply pigeon-holed into 'experienced' and 'inexperienced', however; the scale of operation is relevant. The Developer who produces a single multi-million pound shopping centre every 10 years clearly has experience, and so does a High Street retailer undertaking a dozen £100,000 refurbishment projects each year. The nature of the experience is different, but it would be a mistake to consider either of them to be experienced or naive. It is the appreciation and understanding of what their experience is, and where the limitations of experience are, that are important to the Consultant. All parties must appreciate these issues, if appropriate language is to be used in communication and a true understanding of goals, aspirations and methodology achieved.

Skill base and repertoire

There is concern that experience is an inadequate basis for considering the future. Nutt (1988, p. 130) refers to the need for briefing to acknowledge that current practice is an unreliable guide, to even the medium-term future. Parallel observations noting that Employers' initial goals are often forgotten by the end of a project certainly endorse this view.

Similarly, there is wide acceptance that increasing complexity demands broader skill bases (Becker 1991, p. 26). The Johari window (Figure 4.3) used by Barrett (1995, p. 85) to indicate potential knowledge gaps in the briefing process, shows how knowledge may be withheld or simply be unknown to either party. The level of trust, development of common language and an understanding of all parties' requirements becomes critical, to ensure maximum disclosure and to allow the identification of areas of deficiency within the team as a whole.

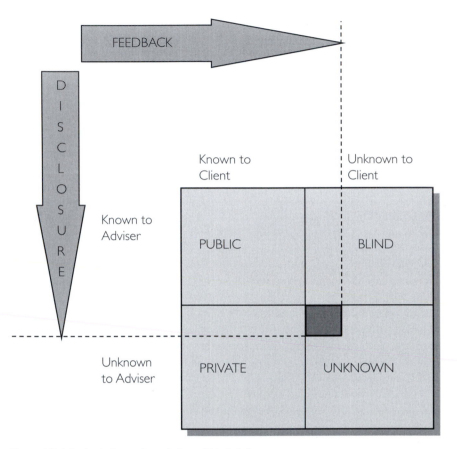

Figure 4.3 Johari window – knowledge within briefing
Source: Barrett 1995a, p. 85.

The background and experience of Consultants and Employers determines, to a large extent, their response to any project (Usmani and Winch 1993, p. 10). Results of a research project undertaken in 1982 (Mackinder and Marvin 1982, p. 1) indicated that initial concepts, building plans, form and general construction are developed rapidly using little information other than the Employer's brief, the site constraints and experience. This pattern of work contrasts with models of theoretical design sequencing.

Where briefing guides, developed by the Designer or Employer are used, it is found (Mackinder and Marvin 1982, p. 4) that these provide a valuable basis for the development of design and also minimise communication problems. There is concern, however, that published Client guidance is slanted in favour of the service provider, and continues to include a high level of technical language (Atkin et al. 1996, p. 13). The Link Construction, Maintenance and Refurbishment (CMR) programme, by Strathclyde University and others (Lupton and Stellakis, p. 49) notes a lack of guidance to achieve *practical* performance.

The conclusion of the above studies is that both Consultants and Employers use experience first and foremost, with reference to written data being a last resort (Mackinder and Marvin 1982, p. 4). Preiser concurs with this view, referring to use by Consultants of 'their own repertoires, supported by their educational background and vocabulary' (Preiser 1993, p. 411).

It is often the case that Employers may be venturing into the unknown, while their advisers and suppliers within the construction industry have 'seen it all before'. In such circumstances experience can clearly be of assistance but equally can be a major obstacle and barrier to innovation, and to the task of determining the Employer's true values and requirements, as opposed to smothering him with preconceived solutions.

The Author's 1998 study responses regarding the basis of briefing (Figure 3.4) reinforces this point. It notes experience as the primary source of knowledge. More disturbingly this remains a constant in many projects, almost regardless of the level of the team's particular experience. The level of genuine research undertaken by most Consultants is minimal, perpetuating the *status quo* and offering little innovation to the Employer's solution. Conversely, it may be argued that Employers producing non-strategic and prescriptive briefs may expect, and deserve, little else.

Practical experience suggests (Richardson 1996, p. 57) that a key question for Employer *and* Consultant should be: 'Are the skills of the other party appropriate to the project in hand?' The criticality of the Employers in the design process is supported by many contributors, but their precise role is subject to debate. Salisbury and White believe the Employer should initiate, instruct and monitor progress, and the Consultant should advise, design and manage activities (Salisbury and White 1980, p. 7). The responsibility for the brief rests with no-one else: 'If the brief is delegated to the Architect, then the client is responsible for examining for compliance' (Salisbury 1998, p. 70). The University of Reading (Gray et al. 1994, p. 20) and O'Reilly (1992, p. 1) agree, concluding: 'Only the client knows what he wants'.

Treading some middle ground, Cuff generally follows this line of thought, noting that the Employer plays an active role with the Consultant giving constraints, advice and approval throughout the process, without which the appropriateness of the service is threatened. She observes from studies that Architects complain about over-active Clients, but there is evidence that the best buildings have Clients who are indeed very active, *but* are also willing to step back at crucial points (Cuff 1996, p. 171).

Conversely Usmani and Winch (1993, p. 57) believe that the briefing problem is largely the responsibility of the Architect. Such differing views imply that practice may be similarly diverse, with disastrous results should the issue not be discussed and team members quietly holding opposing views.

Roles, teams and leadership in practice

The Author's 1998 study sought to determine the composition of teams and to expose potential differences in perception. The comparison of the Consultant's with the Employer's view of 'who's involved' follows a *broadly* similar pattern, but subtle differences are noted leading to a variety of expectations.

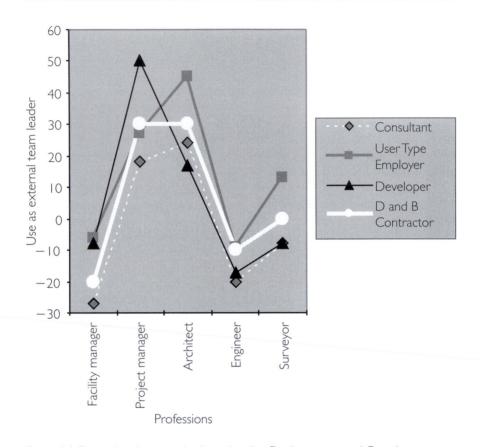

Figure 4.4 External project team leaders related to Employer types and Consultant perception

When considering the external Consultant team it can be seen that user Employers favour the use of an Architect as team leader, whereas Developers are much more likely to appoint a Project Manager. Figure 4.4 demonstrates this view. There is, however, a high correlation between Employers of all sorts and Consultants that Architects are generally the first external profession to be appointed, with between 62 and 69 per cent of projects falling into this pattern.

There is a difference in perception, however, at the stage at which the external design team is appointed. Figure 4.5 indicates this difference. Consultants generally perceive that they are involved earlier in the project process than is the Employer's perception. D and B Contractors tend to concur with the Consultants view of early involvement, again demonstrating the deviation of this Employer group from the 'norm' of their peers.

Most Employers appoint Consultants when they have 'a quantified requirement ... with a draft budget'. The relevance of this, and the Consultant's percep-

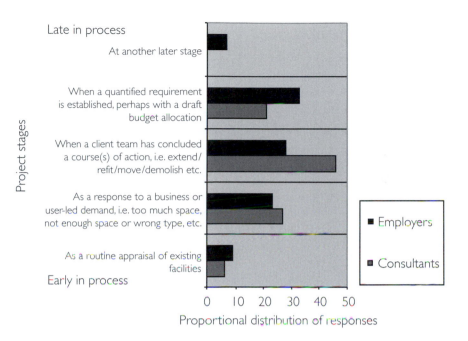

Figure 4.5 Comparative perception of project stage at Consultant appointment

tion that they are embarking upon a project at a much more fluid stage, will be analysed in later chapters.

To assist the understanding of the total project team, Employers were asked whether they considered that the design team as a whole contributes to the development of the brief, other than its interpretation, and if so who contributes the most. A majority of Employers (85 per cent) agreed that the design team does actively contribute to the development of the brief. This contrasted however with the Consultants' view where 46 per cent of respondents believed that as a body they do *not* contribute. However, of those perceiving that the design team do contribute, there was a very strong majority stating that the Architect, as a single profession contributes the most. Again, the implications will be considered in later chapters.

The formation of a project team varies in accordance with the project in hand, and with the Employer's resources/knowledge. Inevitably any project will involve at least one Employer's representative to issue instructions and to provide an information flow. The 1998 survey reveals, within each of the three Employer groups, who is designated to lead the team from the Client's side and who from the Client's side is actively involved. Figure 4.6 summarises the responses in relation to leadership.

Leading the user Employer (of which a high proportion, 71 per cent, are experienced) team, there are estates officers and development managers,

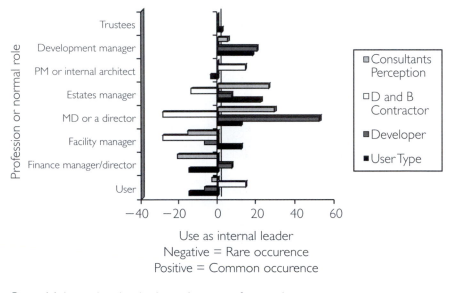

Figure 4.6 Internal project leaders – the range of perception

followed some way behind by facility managers and managing directors. The power structure of many Developers' organisations is revealed, in that it is clearly indicated to be a managing director, or equivalent, who retains a high level of leadership. Supporting this finding a 1989 survey (Franks 1998, p. 56) noted that 100 per cent of Developers retained high level hands-on involvement throughout the project. No other Employer type demonstrates this level of 'hands-on' involvement, and it may in part contribute to a perception of 'value added', as described in Chapter 5.

Responses from Design and Build Contractors again provide a spread of responses from which later interpretation will be made. In general, Consultants support the overall view of the Employer and perceive a managing director (MD) or estates officers to be their normal contact point. It is good to see matching perceptions on at least one point.

The active members in the Employer's internal team shown by the 1998 study follow the patterns in Figure 4.7. The comparison of the Consultants' perception of 'who stays involved' with the Employers' view in Figure 4.7 follows a *broadly* similar pattern. It is noted however that the Consultants perceive MDs and estate managers to remain more active than Employers themselves suggest, probably because they remain the primary contact point with the Consultant principal. The subtle divergence between a role as contact point and a reducing involvement involves inevitable delegation and a management interface within the Employer's organisation.

A further significant difference in perception relates to facility management. Employers have a higher perception of facility management involvement at briefing

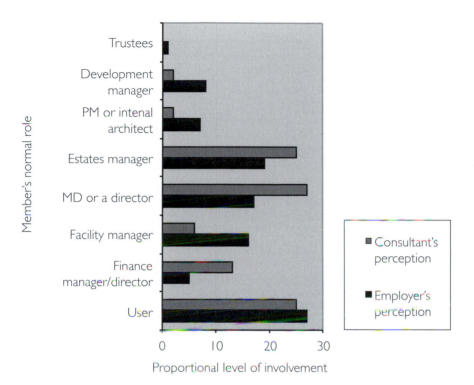

Figure 4.7 Employer's internal team – the perception of active members

stage than do Consultants. The appreciation of the role and the project spread contribute to this gap, which is discussed in later chapters.

In considering space and facility management, McGregor (McGregor and Shiem-Shin Then 1999, p. 56) attempts to define the roles that are involved within any project team. He defines a list of 11 functions:

- leader (Champion);
- facility manager;
- project manager (large projects);
- business planner;
- researcher;
- space planner;
- IT provider;
- customers;
- corporate client;
- implementers;
- property agents;
- Designers and Contractors.

Clearly one would hope that, except for the very largest project, each role would not demand an independent presence, but the point is that to achieve strategic fit with the business, this range of responsibilities and responses is required. Designers have been seen to argue for early involvement; although this has merit, it is very much a clear strategic business objective that is most sought at the outset.

Frequently dissatisfaction stems from failure by Employers to appreciate fully the magnitude of their roles as initiators, information providers, communicators and organisers. However, Murray and Gameson's conclusion that 'effective communication of a brief implies a knowledge that simply may not exist' can often represent the situation for the non-expert (Preiser 1993, p. 430).

In-house appointments for the 'brief writer' have advantages in terms of knowledge of the organisation but the person may be too close to the project and lack both credibility and an overview. Conversely, the appointment of an external Consultant demands a steep learning curve. It also requires an analysis of the prospective project and existing in-house skills to determine the appropriate Consultant.

It is suggested that the majority of successful design projects have been characterised by the maximum possible integration of the Employer into the design team and thus into the process. Some Employers, however, prefer Architects to simply 'get on with the job' (Harwood 1996, p. 9). These same Employers often expect their consultant to have 'psychic' powers to enable them to see both the future and the past!

Many commentators (Franks 1998, p. 7) automatically conclude that the employment of a project manager is essential, without considering the role of that individual and the dynamic of the team as a whole. Project management is not new. It originates in the seventeenth century in what was known as a clerk of works, whose role was to co-ordinate contractors and suppliers of the day. The role of the project manager and the subsequent cost is often seen as a surrogate for Client involvement and as a means of avoiding design team conflict. There is unquestionably a risk associated with the Client stepping back from the project.

One recent study (Somogyi 1999) on the role of project management received an astounding 98 per cent response noting the role as very important. However, the same respondents had a depressing perception of the main contributions of this professional manager. The two highest rated functions included:

1   ensuring that tender documents are appropriately complete for tender;
2   ensuring that design works are appropriately complete before tender.

This clearly demonstrates an element of linear thinking which, although relevant to some projects, would certainly leave many in a state of delay before they started. A little more dynamism should be expected from the project manager, and it should be incumbent upon the best to ensure that Employer expectations are raised a little higher than the two functions above.

Leadership (or 'project management') is accepted as having importance although there is much debate as to the most appropriate party to take on the role. There is an underlying belief that overall project management is not the remit of any particular design team member (Walker 1989, p. 100). This view is also supported by the RIBA, noting that the traditional role of the architect has moved from the project leader to design team leader, leaving ambiguity in its wake (Gray et al. 1994, p. 3). Similarly, Walker expresses concern regarding the traditional management of projects, noting that Architects and Quantity Surveyors do not have the appropriate skills to co-ordinate and manage the total project. He identifies six traditional models for project leaders and their relationship to the team, and then proceeds to identify a further 42 possible organisational structures (Walker 1989, pp. 175–208).

It has been suggested that an integrating agency is essential to avoid layers of interpretation. The Tavistock Institute (1999), in an initial draft consultation paper, has suggested that up to the traditional RIBA stage E the Architect is best placed to integrate (lead) the design team, but management would be better carried out by others. The management is described as dealing with those administrative issues that some Consultants have found unappealing, and have consequently often neglected. The same draft consultative paper considers that Contractors are preferred as managers after stage E, when 'design independencies' are resolved.

There is, therefore, a differentiation between design management and design leadership. Egan (Saxon, *Architects Journal*, 3 February 2000, p. 38) notes that 'nobody is prepared to take responsibility for satisfying the Client'. He argues that the traditional divided role left Clients to their own devices in considering which 'team' member was the most appropriate to manage.

'A wheel of dominance' has been proposed (Gray et al. 1994, p. 23), whereby the team leader is selected by the knowledge level he possesses relative to the stage of the project. Following this logic there is the possibility of changing leadership during the life of the project. This supports the experiments by Fred Fiedler and Bavelas who noted that appropriateness and the level of contribution allowed the natural selection of a leader (Davenport 1994, p. 230). A significant amount of research has been carried out in relation to the dynamics of the project team, and in particular Darnokoff (Cuff 1996, p. 188) examines a conversation between Client, Architect and specialist Contractor. By examining language and protocol, it is demonstrated that language, role, culture, agenda and technicality can quickly become intertwined to produce a highly complex and dynamic situation. The development of task specific systems is an essential solution to harness potential synergy.

The concept of the common goal is an accepted part of good team work. It is also accepted that strategic shift can of course occur and it is the control of such a shift that is a key task (see Figure 3.1) for both the design team leader and the project manager. Information transfer through team leaders can result in unintentional prioritisation and change. 'All team' briefing forums can avoid this but require careful management, again to avoid personal differences in interpretation and a balanced input.

Kolb's learning cycle is well known in demonstrating the sequences of sensing, watching, thinking and doing. However, individual design team members have a variety of perceptions in relation to this process. Powell (Barrett and Males

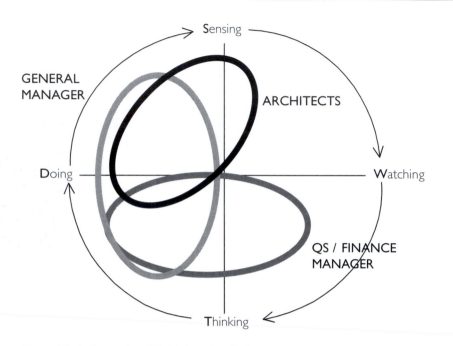

Figure 4.8 A Composite of Kolb's Learning Cycle

1991, pp. 137–48) produces a set of Kolb's learning cycles in respect of a variety of professions to be found within the normal design team. Some are reproduced in Figure 4.8. For the team to function and to achieve any level of 'forming, storming and norming', it is essential that members accept these differences and appreciate the strength of the combination.

Leadership and strategies for resolving potential conflict are considered in later chapters, but trust, equitable motivation and a respect for peers skills that are the clear basis of ensuring reconciliation of these issues to the benefit of the project.

One neglected role of the Employer is their involvement with the service brief *to* the Consultants (not the project brief). All too frequently Consultants embark upon commissions for which there may be a project brief but with no clear understanding of their own and other team members' expected roles (Further Education Funding Council, 1998). The University of Reading research (Gray et al. 1994, pp. 47–9) suggests the use of a start-up meeting at each stage, that is, brief, design and engineering. They propose the use of formal agendas and a presentation by each member about their role, as a method of avoiding conflict. As Pennington (1986, p. 228) notes, failure to clarify roles within a team will inevitably lead to project failures.

The lack of an appropriate service brief and, commonly, any strategic plan compounds the misunderstanding between Consultants and their Employers. Essentially they often embark upon a project already carrying excess baggage and having different start and finish lines. As a means to overcome this in everyday practice, two-way service briefing is suggested and explored in chapter 8.

The role of facility management

Facility management does not have a high profile in literature and research in the context of briefing and design development. The 1998 study supported this view.

Duffy (Preiser 1993, p. 85) notes that it is rare for the role of a facility manager to be explored within the development framework and, conversely, facility managers often have a poor view of Developers. Exceptions include Stockley Park near Heathrow, Broadgate in the City, and Stuart Lipton, the Developer. He formed a 'focus' group that comprised facility management, Users and Consultants, which was highly innovative in 1985. This group concluded that the demand rather than traditional supply is the key issue. Lipton's continued high-level involvement with Governmental initiatives reinforces his belief in the potential for improvement through innovation and effort. The success of Broadgate, from the facility management perspective, is based upon 'the articulate user pressure on design and the persistence of the Developer in closing the feedback loop between those who suffer and those who provide'.

The Library of Congress defines facility management as 'the Practice of co-ordinating the physical workplace with the people and work of the organisation; it integrates the principles of business administration, architecture and the behavioural and engineering sciences' (Kernohan et al. 1996, p. 9). The lack of this integration would appear to be a root cause of many function related failures, referred to elsewhere.

Becker (1991, p. 61) similarly regards the facility manager as having a crucial role in understanding Consultant roles and the anticipated 'deliverables'. He sees facility management as able to identify critical strategic goals and corporate culture. Assessment of risks and benefits, and the production of facility management performance indicators, is considered to be central to the objective assessment of realisation (Becker 1991, p. 262).

There is evidence that the latter qualities are slowly becoming appreciated. The publicity (Cook, Building, 14 August 1998, p. 44) surrounding the PFI (Private Finance Initiative) school in Colfox has referred, in depth, to the role of facility management. To quote the project leader, 'FM has had a massive influence', becoming heavily involved with the design and briefing processes. Critics of such involvement observe that FM leads to blandness; those involved deny this, noting no desire to see innovation stifled. PFI would appear to be one vehicle for raising the profile of FM at design stage.

Where FM continues to be seen as a purely operational expertise, simply demanding zero maintenance, long-life products with no corners or joints and complete repetition of specification, then blandness may well be the order of the day. Those projects using FM in the strategic sense, considering future options, producing a facility brief and reconciling changing and adapting user requirements to a physical form, will see innovation and real management input into projects.

The Author's study found facility management had a low profile in practice, but usually this was admitted by Employers with a tinge of guilt. The Employer advising that his organisation did not have a FM policy in place, and then noticing the BIFM certificate on the wall next to him, typified the dilemma experienced by many. Most Employers accept the benefits of FM despite their lack of action. The 1999 British Institute of Facility Management (BIFM) survey confirms this, noting that 58 per cent of Employers consider FM to have a medium or high strategic importance. It is disappointing therefore that the facility management brief within projects is rarely developed. FM remains misunderstood and a number of Employers persist in considering it to be an 'unavoidable evil'.

Much of the 'confusion' surrounding the role and skills of facility management may well revolve around the issue of identity and definition. The BIFM's own survey includes 30 separate categories of activities undertaken by facility managers as a body. Equal diversity is shown by the same study when considering the background of BIFM members. With a dozen professions represented and 18 qualifications reported, it is not improbable that an Employer will be confused as to the role of facility management. This issue is revisited in Chapter 8, when considering how facility management skills may be maximised by both Consultant and Employer.

User participation

'Empowerment' has become a 'popular' concept, as initiatives such as 'Investors in People' and TQM gain momentum. Improvements in living standards encourage higher standards of expectation amongst employees at all levels. It has been accepted for some years that user involvement improves overall facility satisfaction. (Sources include Hester, Becker (1991, p. 25) and Sanoff (Becker 1991, p. 412).) Furthermore, dissatisfaction amongst users not involved has been well publicised, including the high profile MORI survey finding that 75 per cent of the occupants of the Lloyds building found it unsatisfactory (Becker 1991, p. 26).

Zeisel (1984) has shown gaps (Figure 4.9) that can develop between the paying Client and the End User, and in turn between the End User and the Designer. His diagram could easily be expanded to show gaps that can develop between other stakeholders. In large disparate bodies the use of focus groups can be used as a means of managing data, but this can also allow expectations to develop which go beyond the overall project boundary. Focus groups, in common with any other group, can involve issues of group dynamics and the bias created by dominant voices.

The term 'User' has been defined in the widest context by Bejder (Barrett and Males 1991, p. 126; Becker 1991, p. 125) to include all stakeholders. Using this broad definition, an international research team (Becker 1991, p. 125) in 1983 studied the issue of briefing and concluded that it broke into three stages; they continued to study the effects of User involvement at defined stages. The research concluded that *appropriate* involvement was beneficial, but that the involvement of certain user groups at certain stages could actually be counter-productive.

Allinson (1997, p. 27) graphically demonstrates the natural timing of involvement for any contributor to a project, noting that few can warrant continuous membership of the team. Stakeholder mapping can identify status and involvement, and is used as a graphical technique in Chapter 8. The Designer is a stake-

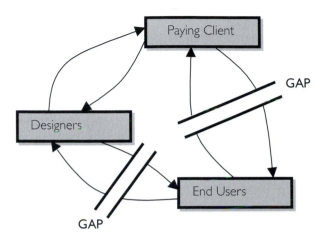

Figure 4.9 The stranded user

holder and as such will always need to maintain a balance between his personal knowledge and his experience as a user himself. It is at this point that culture and background again become major issues.

User involvement can be difficult to achieve, as Kernohan, Gray, Daish and Joiner (1996) suggest. Users may be unknown or transitory, and frequently exhibit different social and cultural characteristics. As a consequence, Developer-type briefs often say little about the practical needs of ultimate users, who may, as yet, be unborn.

The example previously cited, of the Health Authority, demonstrates this point. The Employer/Client body is generally represented by a mixture of contributors involving management, procurement, surgical, nursing, ancillary and support staff. The reconciliation of many different levels of understanding and need is complex. The task of separating the really critical requirements from those perceived as critical by senior management requires significant understanding of the overall organisation, and some sensitivity in addressing internal political issues.

The same scenario is seen in larger projects, where the composition of the team changes as individuals relocate or change roles. The need to adapt to the changing views of the User representative has to be reconciled with the generic User requirement. The ideal of the cyclical brief and design process, in theory, allows continuous change, but in practice demands the establishment of long-stop dates for each element of information. An established, agreed protocol, and a personal understanding of the limitations of individuals is necessary to determine that the User representative is indeed genuinely representing the views of Users in general, and not simply pursuing a personal agenda. Failure to achieve this will result in dissatisfaction for a potentially large and vocal portion of the Employer/Client body.

The 1998 study exposed precisely these problems as a common occurrence. User involvement does not automatically ensure *satisfaction*, but it is argued that User exclusion invariably results in *dissatisfaction*. Case studies (Young 1999) carried out in three major organisations during 1999 showed that although executive sponsorship was evident, User and staff involvement was only noted in the form of post-decision workshops. Such actions do not merit the title of 'involvement'.

Ultimate involvement of the user can be seen in good practice 'Community Architecture', but Jeremy Hill (1998, p. 8) believes that 'community Architecture (often) produces disenfranchisement of both Architect and user'. The issue of balance and appropriateness must always override preconceptions about methodology.

The exploitation of User knowledge in terms of feedback (post-occupancy evaluation) is rare. The University of Reading (1989, p. 66) proposes that readily available and published performance feedback from all new buildings should be available. But, as Barrett (1995, p. 79) observes, even experienced Employers, familiar with briefing and with well developed systems, can fail to optimise user information by not undertaking building evaluations.

The Reading proposals, although commendable, would appear to be distant in realisation. 'Best practice' is seen to utilise post-occupancy evaluations, but frequently these are either limited to internal evaluations that do not involve the Consultant team or, alternatively, are subjective to the extent that they fail to provide explicit information upon which to build a genuine body of knowledge. Tacit information readily available on completion of a project and in the early period of occupancy must be captured and converted into explicit knowledge to the benefit of the entire team. If partnering arrangements are to have any value then it must be this learning process that creates it. Occasional fragmented sources of information exist, but so often to diverse metrics and of ambiguous quality. The management of knowledge is another fundamental element of closing the gap between expectation and realisation.

Summary

It can be seen that the range of issues impinging upon the relationship of the Employer with the Consultant, and consequently on the briefing and design process, is wide and multi-faceted. The list below provides a snapshot of the issues involved:

- motivation;
- language and perception;
- translation (visualisation);
- IT;
- agenda;
- culture;
- multi-headed organisations;
- skill base and repertoire;
- roles, teams and leadership;
- FM role;
- User participation.

To ignore any of these issues carries the risk of creating hurdles to the successful resolution of supply and demand, and consequently expectation and realisation.

The process, already complex, is required to grapple with concepts of quality and a breadth of softer issues beyond the pure physical demands of the brief. The next two chapters consider the results of the 1998 study. The relevance of the impinging issues will become clear, as reasons for perceived failures are described.

5 Sources of failure – results of the 1998 study

Introduction

The Author's research work in 1998, somewhat depressingly for the construction industry, produced results which were similar in terms of distribution and magnitude to surveys completed up to some 20 years ago. Building upon earlier surveys, however, the 1998 study was able to provide a greater breadth and subtlety of response, providing greater insights in to the root of the problem. During interviews virtually all of the impinging issues described in Chapters 2, 3 and 4 are evident. It is for this reason that the problem and consequent solution need to be seen as a performance gap which is very much multi-faceted.

Current initiatives provide a 'feel good' factor for the industry as a whole. Partnering arrangements, for example, have led many to believe that change has really occurred. Change is occurring in 'best' practice, but everyday common practice, of which we are all party to at some time, leaves much to be desired. This chapter summarises the levels of failure in practice, and provides a sharp antidote to any complacency.

Surprisingly some Employers, including those considered to be experienced, noted that they had no knowledge of areas of failings or levels of satisfaction. It is also clear, although not surprising, that many Consultants fail to carry out any objective evaluation of their completed projects. As described earlier, the existence of post-occupancy evaluations or even a simple telephone call, beyond the 'defects' period, is rare. Is it fear, lack of interest or perpetuation of the 'one-off' culture? Most Employer feedback related to consistent failings regarding time and finance, closely followed by quality. Repetitive reference is made by numerous respondents to the lack of understanding by someone within the project team as a whole, whether Employer or Consultant.

Consultants feel strongly that lack of understanding and their inability to become involved at the earliest possible stage are the key reasons for failures in the design arena. Figure 4.5 clearly shows the difference of opinion between Employers and their Consultants as to the stage of the project at which they are appointed.

Despite the acknowledged appointment of the Architect, closely followed by the Project Manager, as the first Consultants to a project team, it is clear that neither have any significant involvement in assessing need. The strategic issues involved prior to commitment to many everyday projects are subject to little objective assessment. Clearly many major projects, and particularly those undertaken by Developers, are evaluated much more rigorously in relation to a very specific range of criteria. It would appear, however, that in common practice this is the exception rather than the rule.

Concern is also expressed by several respondents that too frequently the 'bottom line' is the driver, rather than quality. Certainly the emphasis on finance in the Employers' comments confirmed this is a high priority and a potentially high-risk area. The resultant lack of design development is commonly cited as a source of failing. The sentiment is similarly supported by many Consultants. The Government edict requiring public sector departments to achieve procurement by 'best value' techniques, as opposed to compulsory competitive tendering, by 2004 has the potential to change this driver. The issues discussed in Chapters 2, 3 and 4 are very much the agenda of everyday Employers and Consultants. However the hurdle of 'cost' in the tournament of quality equals remains. Employers have to determine how much 'development' they can afford to buy. Chapter 6 considers responses, together with the wider issues associated with 'value'.

A clear lack of trust between parties working towards a common goal remains evident. It is hardly a basis for successful performance in a project. Initial project team meetings often discuss issues of open communication, shared goals and so on, promptly to return home and produce double sets of cost plans and programmes. Interview comment confirms this is still a fact of common practice and no myth. Supply Chain Networking, Prime Contracting and 'Partnering' are all responses to this issue and are discussed at length in Chapter 7. Current common practice is a long way below these ideals. This chapter and Chapter 6 show that the attitudes of all parties require overhaul.

At the more subjective level of functionality and aesthetics, there remains throughout the design industries an agenda that seeks to push the Client as far as possible to produce an 'architectural statement'. In parallel, the Client seeks to achieve business plan objectives, while cost Consultants and Contractors aim to comply with original estimates. Impinging issues include the question of who judges success and by what criteria.

As Employer respondents observed, it is frequently little things that have a major effect upon perception. One exceptional Employer noted that '10 per cent failure is reasonable, only non-building people expect better, they don't understand that each is a prototype'. This was a view diametrically opposed to the Egan report, published just six weeks after this comment! Perhaps attitudes, and not systems, need the upgrade.

Methodology

The initial study itself was undertaken over a 9 month period during 1998. It started as research for a Dissertation produced as part of a Masters Degree, but it soon became clear that the subject was critical to both the author's business and that of his Clients. The combination of academic and practice based-research provided an excellent basis on which to seek out data and opinions only alluded to in many guides and 'initiatives'.

Responses span a hard-to-soft spectrum as referred to in Chapter 1; scales were therefore devised to allow for comparison of data at the softer end, together with questions to allow the assessment of weighting. The questionnaire followed the form and structure described previously. As noted, where subjective terms were used, they were given quantum by reference to a percentage or other relevant hard figure.

The presentation of the results shows hard figures where appropriate, but generally relates responses on a proportional basis, which is considered more relevant than the use of absolute numerical results. Issues that invited multiple responses at either end of a scale, i.e. common and rare, are represented on single charts with the convention of 'positive' indicating the degree of normality (common) and 'negative' indicating the degree of rarity.

The charts reproduced in preceding chapters described survey responses in the form of raw data or facts, for comparison with the existing body of knowledge. This chapter aims to interpret the raw data and provide some explanation of the anomalies and trends that research revealed.

Respondent profile

Questionnaires were returned from a wide range of Employers and Consultants, covering the following generic fields:

- NHS Trusts;
- private manufacturing PLCs and limited companies (regional, national and international);
- charitable organisations;
- retailers (regional, national and international);
- further and higher educational establishments;
- private developers (commercial, industrial and retail; regional and national);
- private commercial businesses, i.e. finance, insurance;
- housing associations;
- Design and Build Contractors (regional, national and international);
- local authorities;
- government departments and quangos;
- telecommunications;
- hotel and leisure PLCs and limited companies;
- Consultants (all disciplines: see Figure 5.2).

The Employer responses can be further subdivided, as below:

User Type	73 per cent
Developer	17 per cent
Design and Build Contractor	10 per cent

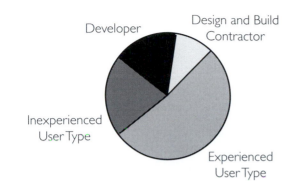

Figure 5.1 The composition of Employer respondents

Respondent definition, explained in Chapter 1, is summarised below for convenience:

- 'User type Employer' – Employers commissioning design and construction works for their own direct use, such as manufacturers, retailers, health trusts;
- 'Developer' – Procurer of the design and construction of facilities on behalf of others, either on a speculative basis or in conjunction with a specific tenant/purchaser;
- Design and Build Contractors can be found as part of the procurement path for either 'User' or Developer Employers. The nature of D and B however is such that the Contractor is frequently an Employer of design teams in a similar way to the other Employer groups.

By their very nature Developers and Design and Build Contractors can be described as experienced, 'sophisticated' Employers, familiar with the construction; and design industry. Conversely, user Employers may have infrequent demands to procure design or construction, respondents have therefore been subdivided as follows:

1   experienced Clients – who have a repetitive construction programme and employ staff expressly for procurement and liaison with external consultants – normally professionals themselves;
2   inexperienced Clients – who have infrequent design/construction demand and have little or no relevant knowledge.

Of the User Employer respondents, 29 per cent fall in to the category of 'inexperienced'. Figure 5.1 graphically describes the employer population. The range of respondents was particularly wide, and this in turn was reflected in the project range. The variety of responses added colour and diversity, but also gave sufficient range to allow the extraction of the 'normal'.

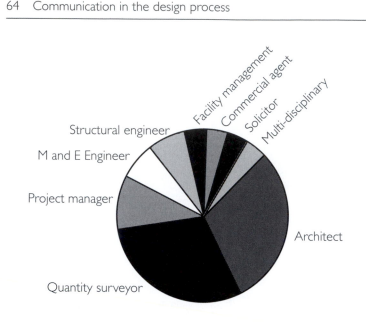

Figure 5.2 Disciplines of Consultant respondents

The range of projects, in terms of numbers initiated per annum, varies from 1 to 120. The mean average for the three sectors of Employers is as follows:

- User type Employer – mean average 18 projects per annum;
- Developer type Employer – 9;
- Design and Build Contractor (as Employer) – 27.

Design and Build contractors were unanimous in agreeing that their projects were particularly diverse, which reflects the variety of sectors within which most work. The highest level of repetition was indicated, not unsurprisingly, within the user Employer, where 29 per cent of respondents believe that over $\frac{3}{4}$ of their projects were repetitive. Similarly, Developers tend to specialise in a sector and have a high level of repetition.

The Consultant responses represent a variety of disciplines, as indicated in Figure 5.2, and show a range of project type repetition reflecting the specialisms that some organisations have, with the diversity that others have chosen.

Levels of failure between expectation and realisation

The survey and interviews were based upon the subdivision of information flow into four briefs, namely function, finance, timescale and aesthetics, the latter being determined by pre-study interviews and reference to previous studies. As previously noted, the choice of the first three is supported by survey work completed by numerous other sources (Barrett and Males 1991, p. 176; Preiser 1993, p. 432;

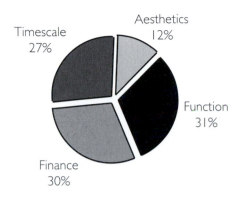

Timescale
27%

Aesthetics
12%

Function
31%

Finance
30%

Figure 5.3 Relative weighting of failure areas

Walker 1989, p. 70), and it was felt inappropriate to ignore aesthetics in the design context. The potential commodity value of aesthetics can indeed have a bearing upon financial appraisal (Allinson 1997, p. 13).

The relative weighting of failure areas as shown by this survey and indicated by Figure 5.3 confirms that function, finance and timescale are the predominant concerns of Employers. As one interviewee noted, users are ambivalent about aesthetics. Allinson (1997, p. 17) notes that even 'clients who want dreams are increasingly dominated by time and budgetary constraints'. Therein lies one of the inherent conflicts in almost any procurement: the only too human desire to procure a Rolls at the price of a Mini.

The issues of cost were high on the agenda of most Employers interviewed. This was similarly evident in the comments included on questionnaires. There were concerns that 'the level playing field' meant that price was frequently the main criterion for selection. As previously discussed, when quality is equal, often little is left other than cost. It is perhaps at this point that Employers and Consultants should both turn to the softer cultural issues. The ability to agree completely on the perception of 'value' and to be 'as one' on the 'how' issues must clearly carry a significant financial reward.

The results of the 1998 survey questionnaires broadly produce a normal distribution of failure levels, with the highest incidence of failure falling in the '1–10 per cent of projects' band. This failure band accounts for between 35 and 40 per cent of all responses across all four briefs. Figure 5.4 profiles the perceived failure level across all briefs.

The responses indicated in Figure 2.5 show a curious increase at the highest level of dissatisfaction (60 per cent+), particularly under the briefs of function, finance and timescale. These fall outside of the normal distribution. Much of the contribution to this response level is derived from Developers. Their responses follow a normal distribution over the first three lower bands of dissatisfaction, but it was then found that 10 per cent+ of their responses account for the 60 per cent+ failure level band. It is suggested that some Developer responses are biased

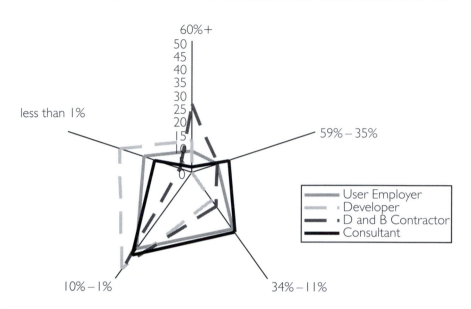

Figure 5.4 Comparison of Employer groups and Consultants – Profile of perceived failure

by their particular sensitivity to short-term goals. With limited exceptions, Developers frequently sell on developments on completion to long-term funding organisations such as insurance and pension funds. In this scenario, Developers as an Employer are particularly sensitive to short-term project performance for the achievement of their financial goals.

The perception of expectation against realisation and consequent failure rates from Consultants follow a similar pattern to the Employers in total, and shows a good normal distribution. It is noteworthy, however, that performance under individual briefs does vary somewhat to Employers, showing that Consultants perceive greater failure rates in terms of timescale. It was noted by more than one interviewee that it has become policy for some Employer organisations to add a contingency timescale (and a financial provision) to targets and programmes given by their Consultants, based upon experience of frequent underestimation. Thus there are two timescales in operation, one being known only to the Employer, resulting in a differing perception of performance. This game of 'cat and mouse' continues to be played not only in the arena of cost and time, but also in respect of aesthetic and functional design, as both parties endeavour to achieve their goals. Genuine 'partnering' scenarios demand an 'open-book' environment that is far removed from current practice.

Failure considered in relation to the type of client and the level of experience

The survey population was random but 29 per cent of the responses were noted as falling within the category of 'inexperienced'. This closely accords with the

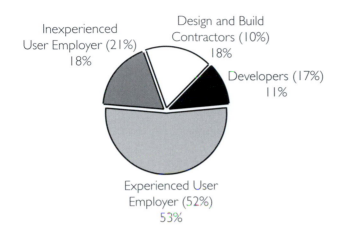

Inexperienced
User Employer (21%)
18%

Design and Build
Contractors (10%)
18%

Developers (17%)
11%

Experienced User
Employer (52%)
53%

Figure 5.5 Sources of failure levels of over 35 per cent in one or more briefs
(bracketed figures are percentage of survey population)

HMSO professional liability study (Gray *et al.* 1994, p. 3) which notes that experienced Clients account for over 75 per cent of situations. Analysis of the sources of significant failure (over 35 per cent of projects) was shown in Figure 2.10, and for convenience reproduced here as Figure 5.5 with the inclusion of the relative percentage of respondents.

Curiously of those respondents reporting failure rates of this level or more, only 18 per cent were inexperienced Employers, despite this group accounting for 21 per cent of respondents. Although the figures are marginal, this does suggest that inexperienced Clients have proportionally less failure than others. There may be three reasons for this apparent inconsistency:

1   By virtue of being inexperienced there is a much lower number of projects upon which their response is based.
2   As an inexperienced Client, their aspirations and expectations *may* be lower.
3   Having little experience, there is evidence that they plan well ahead and take great care in selection of Consultants in whom they place significant trust, and they are risk adverse.

The suggestion that such Clients may have lower expectation is contrary to a comment by another experienced respondent, suggesting that only 'non-building people' would expect failure rates lower than 10 per cent.

Interviews suggest that it is the pre-planning time that bears fruit and allows them to consider all of the strategic options open to their business, and to question fully and understand the commitment that is being undertaken. (See Figure 5.6.) The latter point was endorsed by several responses from the 'inexperienced' group who took great care in pointing out that they spent many, many months

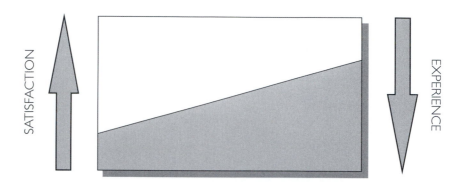

Figure 5.6 Apparent inconsistency

considering the project before any third party was approached. This apparent inconsistency is worthy of note.

Experienced User Employers having 35 per cent+ failure rates are directly proportional to the total respondent population, suggesting that as a body they neither disproportionately add to nor hinder the process.

Developers have a 'good' or lower proportional representation in this result, despite having a high proportional response to the 60 per cent+ classification. Based upon the overall result it is suggested that Developers 'add value' to the process. There are, however, concerns as to how realistically some Developers assess success. This is attributed to this group's high sensitivity to contractual targets, combined with lack of appreciation of any significant failings by Users or subsequent managers. Detailed responses will be considered later.

Design and Build procurement methodology is very much a keystone of a Latham/Egan concept. The integration of construction and design is commendable but is fraught with difficulties. Survey responses included 10 per cent Design and Build Contractors, and yet 18 per cent of 'high failure' responses were attributed to this Employer group. The culture of both Consultants and Contractor can lead to some turbulent projects. Later chapters provide case study and discussion of Design and Build as a possible innovation to improve project quality. The implications of the survey response requires, however, immediate comment.

Anomalies of design and Build contractor responses

Responses from Design and Build Contractors have, throughout the survey, tended to exhibit results outside of the normal pattern. Their view of who leads their team (Figure 4.6) and their agreement with the Consultants' responses, as opposed to the Employers' responses in Figure 4.5 (the appointment stage), is explained, in part, by the diversity of their relationships. It was clear from interviews and meetings as well as questionnaire responses, that Design and Build Contractors, although very much an Employer of Consultants, do not see themselves primarily in this role.

The D and B Contractor finds itself offering an interface role, 'a one stop

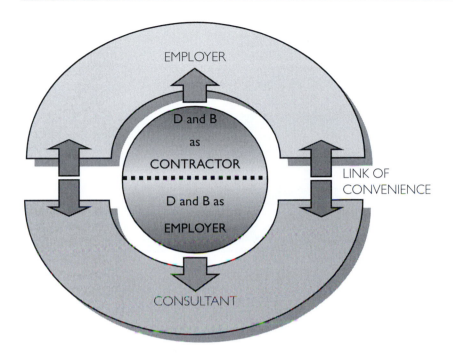

Figure 5.7 Design and Build Contractor interfaces

shop', in which the Consultants are distanced from the ultimate Employer, or User. In response to questioning, however, the Contractors are unclear of their role as Employers, and still tend to respond in Contractor terminology. It was also clear that between different Design and Build Contractors there is a significant variation in the service expected from Consultants, and the way in which projects are managed. The link of convenience shown in Figure 5.7 is a common occurrence and leads to ambiguity. The distinction in roles indicated by the dotted black line in the diagram is far from clear in practice.

In terms of the specific reference to high levels of failure rate, it is believed that the failure rate of their projects as an Employer of Consultants is confused with their role as Contractor to a superior Employer. Many concerns and complaints of this Employer group turned out to refer, on further probing, to their relationship with the ultimate User Employer and not to their own role as an Employer. It is therefore felt that the confusion of roles and the lack of clarity in terms of briefing and management structure exacerbates the variety of exceptional responses from Design and Build respondents.

Although Design and Build has clearly been part of the construction industry for many years, it is considered under Chapter 7 as an alternative initiative in terms of its response to the Egan/Latham challenge.

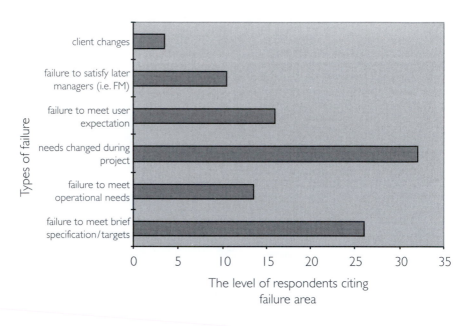

Figure 5.8 Generic areas of failing – The total brief

The nature of failures

The survey data contained in previous chapters and the previous summary firmly establish that there is a gulf between expectation and realisation, which correlates with other studies, and is significant. Despite some respondents having little knowledge of failings, and others thinking that 10 per cent failure was 'OK', most participants in the study were clearly concerned by any failure. The majority of participants certainly aim to achieve improvement.

Taking the brief as a total entity, Figure 5.8 graphically illustrates the main generic areas of failing. All respondent groups are consistent in agreeing that the primary cause of failure can be described as:

- 'Needs changed'.

Other significant causes include:

- failure to meet the agreed brief/specification;
- failure to meet user expectation;
- failure to satisfy subsequent managers, such as facility management;
- failure to meet operational needs.

Breaking down the brief into the four constituents used in the survey, Figure 5.9 shows in detail the allocation of attributed failure areas. Not surprisingly, failures in

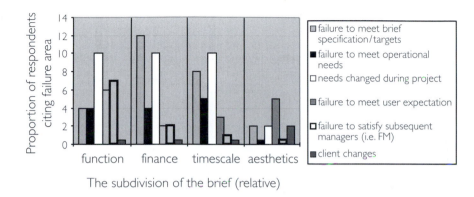

The subdivision of the brief (relative)

Figure 5.9 Generic areas of failing

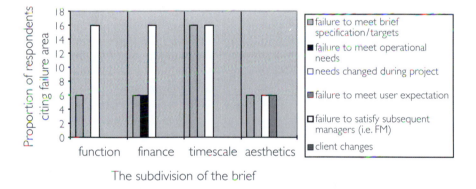

The subdivision of the brief

Figure 5.10 Generic areas of failing – Developers' view

the area of user expectation fall predominately within the functional and aesthetic briefs, whereas failures for subsequent managers are concentrated in the functional brief.

Overall the response between Employer types was generally consistent, with the exception of the Developer who, as previously noted, did not perceive any failure to satisfy subsequent managers. The Developers' view is expressed by Figure 5.10. This is not to suggest that Developers do not care about users or subsequent managers, but merely that the procurement methodology with which they are involved often precludes any direct relationship. Developers seeking to genuinely improve quality of the built environment need to establish sophisticated communication routes beyond the normal tentative linear routes, via a string of Agents, development managers and project managers.

Across all four briefs, therefore, the primary generic areas of failing quoted by respondents are summarised in Figure 5.11.

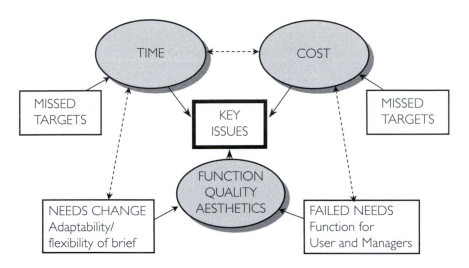

Figure 5.11 Primary areas of failure

It has been noted (O'Reilly 1992, p. 1) that 'only the client knows what he wants', and conversely it has been suggested that the 'original goals are frequently forgotten by the end of the project' (Gray et al. 1994, p. 23).

Undoubtedly both contradictory suggestions are correct. The Employer as a total entity knows what his business requires, strategically and operationally. The difficulty is providing an appropriately weighted and comprehensive statement of what this demand is, and then conveying it, without distortion, to a third party. 'Goals forgotten' clearly do exist, but it is suggested that more often this is a function of a strategy that was embarked upon, but that did not adequately address risks of time and change. This is often exacerbated by diverse demands of site acquisition, planning and construction procurement.

From interview and questionnaire comment, it is clear that change is inevitable during the project procurement period, particularly for major projects and extended timescales. It is also clear that much comment has been made both by respondents of this survey and by other sources, including the recent Egan Report, noting a common failure to provide adequate time for initial development of the brief, establishment of an appropriate information flow and exploration of design options.

Several respondents confirmed that they were conscious of unreasonable demands being imposed on both finance and timescale. The reconciliation of time needed for briefing and design development is essential, as the commercial agenda demands higher efficiency; this reconciliation has to be achieved if the performance gap is to be closed. The quality of time has to be considered in relation to appropriate use. Chapter 8 considers strategies that allow Employers and Consultants alike to squeeze more from the precious time available.

Latham and others suggest that the integrated design team (Design and Build) has a greater potential for efficiency and for the realisation of the goals set by Egan, in respect of cost, timescale and quality. Some respondents, however, note concerns that 'Design and Build' frequently is a means of reducing design development time and, if not appropriately managed at the outset, has a potential for a more significant gap between expectation and realisation. Successful use of this procurement route was generally observed within more experienced organisations. 'Best' practice Design and Build has the capability to deliver a high level of design and finished product but, as previously noted, common practice creates many confused interfaces and complications. We return to this issue in Chapter 7.

The primary reason for project failure is attributed to 'needs change during the project'. It is suggested this category of failure is, in part, a euphemism for elements not appropriately considered at the outset. To 'appropriately consider' an element of the project does not mean, for example, defining every last component and producing the prescriptive specification. 'Appropriate consideration' may mean that an element is not critical to the design and procurement path, and therefore need not be considered at this time. Alternatively, it may be that it is an element possibly subject to future change, in which case the design should adopt the 'loose fit approach' to allow a variety of future options. 'Needs change' so often means elements forgotten, or over-designed and prescriptively specified.

The levels of failure experienced under the aesthetic brief are low. Of those noted, 'failure to meet user expectation', is the highest level. It has been shown from numerous sources outlined in Chapter 4 that user involvement can have a positive effect on eventual satisfaction. This study also shows a high level of user involvement during the briefing stage within user Employer types. It is curious therefore that in the area of aesthetics, their involvement does not appear to reflect this view. Opinions of aesthetic performance viewed from five perspectives, however, showed a high level of correlation, with a large majority of respondents concluding that internal and external appearance fell into the category 'good'.

Only a very small percentage of Consultants and user type Employers responded at the negative end of the scale, i.e. disappointment. As shown by Figure 5.12 disappointment is restricted to the categories of 'acceptance by users' and 'image for business'. The determination of 'who is the Client?' is clearly a major issue for any supplier, and certainly no less for the design team. The balance to be achieved between the Employer requiring a simple weather-proof cover for his manufacturing process, and the demands of the local community for example, is a commonplace dilemma. Its resolution is perhaps one of the major values that the Architect 'brings to the table'.

It is suggested that communication and perception is the key in this situation. It has been demonstrated by a number of sources, including Whorf (Davenport 1994, p. 156), Gameson (Barrett and Males 1991, p. 168) and Winer (Pennington 1986, p. 171), that words and drawings may not be sufficient to truly communicate intentions. This arose several times in interviews; in one situation, an experienced Consultant observed, he had been surprised at a recent interior design scheme when he saw it on site for the first-time. He concluded that the User/Employer had 'no chance of knowing what he was getting'. The aesthetic brief is observed by some respondents to be rarely included; others indicate that the end user is simply indifferent to the finished aesthetic appearance!

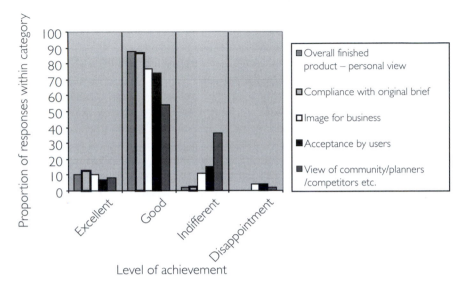

Figure 5.12 Employer view of aesthetic performance

'The user' also rates reasonably high in terms of lack of satisfaction concerning the functional brief. Again, it can be concluded that *involvement* in the briefing stage and with the design team is not sufficient to ensure understanding of the project as designed by the professional third party. This is an issue to be addressed by both Employer and Consultant. The Employer's project sponsor or team leader has a core objective to ensure that all factions of his organisation are appropriately represented. This involves the careful weighting of their views and balancing them against the strategic needs of the business and the project in hand.

It is similarly critical for Consultants to ensure that they have been honestly understood. Readers may be familiar with the feeling of relief experienced when presented proposals are accepted. The 'we got it past them' approach is, however, not good enough. Painful as it may be, it is essential to ensure that even the most reticent of those present has fully 'bought into' the proposal and understands the implications. The failure to have a full understanding, from inception onwards, will always threaten failure.

Within the functional brief, again, a significant failure to meet the requirements of subsequent managers, such as facility management is perceived. The questionnaire indicates that Employers felt facility management was, at a modest level, actively involved with the briefing process. The Consultants' view was that they are rarely involved. Interviews and subsequent meetings tended to endorse the Consultants' view.

Employers interviewed ranged from multinational private to local public sector organisations, but facility management was very low profile in all situations. In only one situation was any level of facility management evident at the briefing stage. A number of other organisations were embarrassed that this was the case. Most supported the concept of FM involvement to inform issues such as whole life

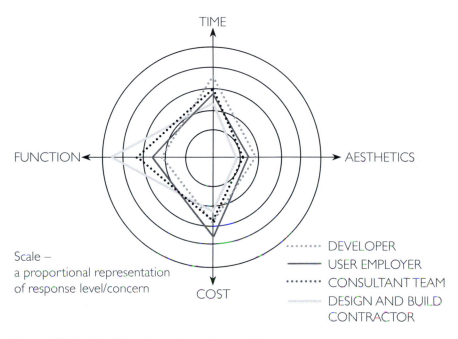

TIME

FUNCTION

AESTHETICS

Scale –
a proportional representation
of response level/concern

COST

·········· DEVELOPER
————— USER EMPLOYER
·········· CONSULTANT TEAM
————— DESIGN AND BUILD
CONTRACTOR

Figure 5.13 Profile of the primary focus of respondent groups

design, adaptability, sustainability and maintainability. However, no organisations interviewed had the appropriate resources or structure to include this in their internal design team. Interpretation suggests that 'property people' within experienced user Employers can see the benefit of an FM approach, but that the idea has yet to be sold to the 'paymaster'.

Failure to meet timescale targets is clearly the major concern of Developers, but it is also of importance to subsequent managers. It is the same problem, but with different motivators. Developers concern with timescale is predominately driven by contractual agreement. Delay for a subsequent manager, i.e. facility management, means a problem elsewhere, typically storage of major plant identified by one interviewee, or temporary accommodation.

From the survey data, a profile, as shown in Figure 5.13, is produced demonstrating the trends of concern of different parties. The focus of each party tends to reflect the concerns discussed above. The Consultants' profile emphasises time, cost and function, in parallel to other groups, which is contrary to many criticisms of the professions. Initially, it might be thought that the balance of professions in the respondent group is responsible for the profile; however, inspection of individual responses shows that the profile matches all separate professions, as well as the team as a whole. The sample is too small to infer significance to this, other than noting that the Architects and other professions surveyed do not exhibit the much criticised characteristics described by the RIBA strategic survey, and others in a similar vein. Other groups show a focus in keeping with general expectation.

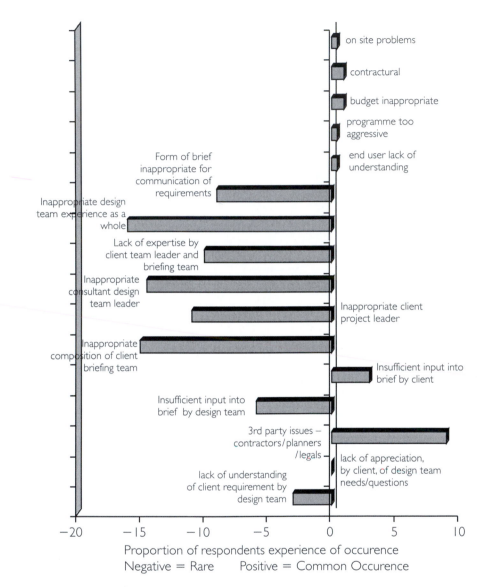

Figure 5.14 Employers' perception of failure causation

Reasons for failures

Employer respondents identified the same reasons for the generic failings as Consultants, noting that most failings are due to third party issues, such as contractors, planners, regulators and legal issues. Third parties were not invited to respond, as it was felt that there would be a certain *déjà vu* in the response. It will be seen that in reality third party issues are not in themselves the underlying reasons for failure. Responses are represented graphically in Figure 5.14.

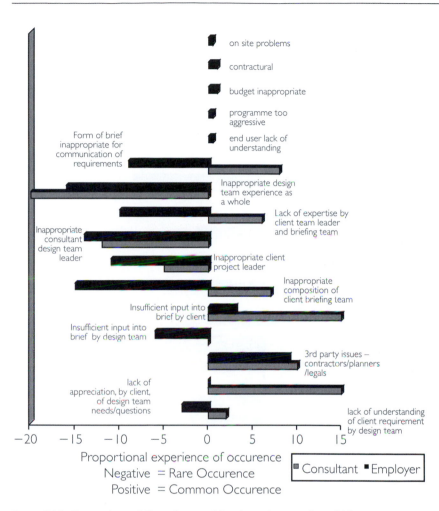

Figure 5.15 Comparison of Consultant and Employers' perception of failure causation

Detailed comparison of Consultants' and Employers' responses, however, begins to reveal some significant differences in perception. Figure 5.15 compares the responses of Consultants with those of Employers. Disparity includes the following reasons that Consultants consider are common failures, but Employers consider to be rare:

- lack of appreciation by Client of design team needs;
- insufficient input into brief by Client;
- inappropriate composition of Client briefing team;
- lack of expertise of Client team leader and briefing team;
- form of brief inappropriate for the communication of requirements.

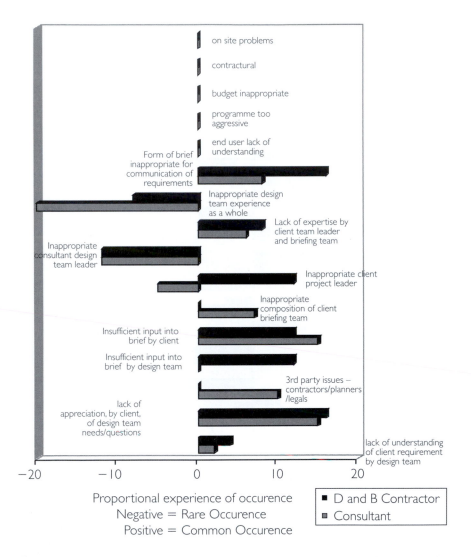

Figure 5.16 Comparison of Consultant and D and B Contractors' perception of failure causation

At a modest level, Consultants conceded there was a lack of understanding of Client requirements by the design team. Employers were modestly self critical of their own level of input into the brief, but considered that the other suggested reasons for failure included on the questionnaire occurred rarely.

Again, the Design and Build Employer results follow more closely the pattern of the Consultants' responses than other Employer groups, as shown in Figure 5.16. Reasons have been proposed previously; nevertheless, this consistent difference in perception does little to dispel assertions from many User Employers regarding 'collusion' between Contractors and Consultants.

The comparison shown in Figure 5.15 clearly demonstrates Consultants' concern that Employers fail to resource adequately and appropriately their own internal teams at the briefing stage. This was not a view held with any great strength by Employers and not evident in interviews and meetings. The interviewees maintained a concern regarding briefing and appreciated the need to provide necessary information. However, they frequently concentrated on specifics and detail, which it would appear were then unquestioningly accepted by the Consultant. This is evidenced by the responses to the questions regarding the level of input into the brief. Consultants' responses indicated that they had a low input into the development of the brief, which contradicted the Employers' view that they in fact had a higher input. This may suggest that Employers believe that their Consultants are actively reviewing instructions and information flow, whereas in fact they appear to be accepting it as a 'fait accompli'.

Consultant respondents repetitively emphasised the view that the time allowed for the preparation of an appropriate brief is being continuously eroded. One respondent despairingly concluded that there is 'rarely a brief at all'.

Certainly this can often be the case with Design and Build Employers, as evidenced previously. Consultants feel strongly that lack of understanding and their inability to get involved at the earliest possible stage are the key reasons for failures in the design arena. Common sense would suggest that involvement of all parties as early as possible should convey benefits to a project. Common sense would also suggest that all parties to a project should work with the same data. Under the guise of 'commercial confidentiality', however, many Consultants and indeed Employers' representatives are working in the dark.

There is also concern that although, as shown in Figure 4.5, Consultants do believe that they are involved earlier than is often the case, they still seem to treat far too much as 'fact'. In order, therefore, to benefit from earlier involvement, the Consultants' bland approach of simply 'accepting the brief' must change. It is at this point that we return to resourcing and the value placed by Employers on this involvement and design development in general.

The apparent speed with which Employers often move to 'solutions' and detailed design reinforces the view that design development is not a significant issue, and yet lack of development is often cited as a failing in service. Figure 5.17 shows the typical distribution of such Employers' effort at project inception. Figure 5.17 also demonstrates the low profile attributed to the service briefing of Consultants, which was acknowledged by a number of interviewees as a neglected area.

Service briefing simplistically relates to the brief that exists, or should exist, between the Employer and Consultant. Emphasis has traditionally been placed upon the project brief. Although this is undeniably important, it would appear equally important to ensure that those persons within the Employer's team and the Consultant's team have a clear understanding of what is expected of them as they endeavour to deliver the demands of the project brief. It should also be emphasised that in addition to the 'what', the 'how' is crucially important if satisfaction is to be achieved by all parties.

Consultants are too often likely to enter into service contracts with Employ-

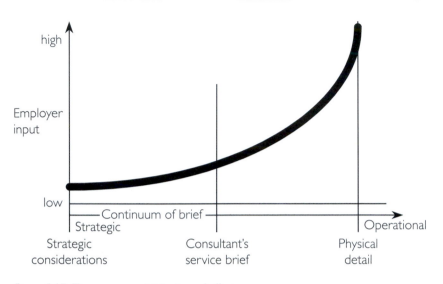

Figure 5.17 The common distribution of effort

ers where both parties believe their respective roles to be clear, but invariably both parties will have different perceptions. Despite improvements in service briefing, many readers will be familiar with the kind of debate that often takes place at a first design team meeting. Consultants are often seen to attempt to pass on tasks to another Consultant, in a general scramble either to avoid or to pick up the pieces of service that potentially may fall into the 'brief' of any one of several Consultants. Typically, simple mechanical tasks, such as drainage design, statutory authority liaisons, contractor interviews, and production of procurement package, can all be reasonably allocated to at least one profession. If Consultants have difficulty determining their task at such a simple mechanical level, then it can be seen why essential but more complex tasks relating to leadership, communication strategies, and management structures are neglected, or at best confused. It was observed during interviews that the scenario described above is indeed commonplace, as Consultants repeatedly embark upon projects with little clear idea of the roles they are to perform.

The question of roles and the desirable input to the early stages of the project by the Employer has been extensively referenced in Chapter 4. The literature shows a mixture of views, one of which indicates that the Consultants should be heavily involved with the development of the brief and another (Gray et al. 1994, p. 20) that briefing is entirely the Employers' responsibility. From questionnaire and interview responses, it would appear that the surveyed Employers believe that the latter is not the case.

Employers, in general, readily walk away from projects at key stages when Consultants are appointed. The delegation of this lead role has been seen to have catastrophic results, particularly in terms of cost and timescale, when sporadic involvement of the Employer demands a change of direction for the project. The latter may be required by what are effectively step changes to the Employer's requirements, but more frequently it is essentially a drift that has occurred during interpretation by the design team.

The gap between Employers' and Consultants' perception of the causes of failure must be closed immediately if, jointly, improvements are to be made. 'No blame' post-occupancy evaluations should become regular occurrences rather than an aspect of best practice only. Current practice occasionally incorporates post-occupancy evaluations, but unfortunately these are often undertaken in the name of Quality Assurance project reviews. The use of a few shallow and stilted questions may satisfy the demand of the checklist, but does little to genuinely improve knowledge in the broadest sense.

Undoubtedly both Employers and Consultants seek to produce briefing documentation of the highest quality, and to ensure that the design process pro-vides for the production of an ever improving product. However, as long as Employers and Consultants have different views on the causes of failure, it is unlikely that major improvement is achievable. Acceptance by both parties of the need to change their role and view of their essential input is necessary.

Resourcing and information

Many studies and guides including the latest Egan report acknowledge the resourc-ing of the early stages of a project to be critical. There may be a certain bias in the Consultants' view that Employers neglect this stage, but this does not lessen the criticality of the task. Numerous sources (Barrett 1995a, p. 80; Nutt 1993, pp. 28–32; Salisbury and White 1980, p. 18; Walker 1989, p. 76) agree that brief-ing is much more than a single static document and that it is reasonably described as an 'information flow'. The way in which this information flow is addressed in practice is simplistic; with the exception of targets for time and finance, the com-monest form of briefing is a verbal meeting. Public sector and more highly experi-enced repeat Employers tend to use more prescriptive written statements: standard specifications and room data sheets are common.

At the other end of the spectrum are 'wish lists', which are frequently employed by public sector organisations having a high level of user involvement. Although such lists are accepted for what they are, they impose a burden of judgement and balance on the Consultant team. This clearly can cause User dis-satisfaction, as evidenced previously under the issues of function and aesthetics. Guidance from the Construction Industry Board and similar recent guidance notes embody good practice comment for Employers, but frequently suggest that brief-ing is a one-off operation, a single stage as demonstrated in the RIBA work plan. In practice, the use of loop briefing techniques, or phasing, to allow a general increase in detail from strategy to micro detail, is not evident.

The common expectation, 'as much information at an early stage', is unfor-tunately normal practice. Even where information is produced in stages, there is little objective strategy associated with the definition of these stages. It is quite normal for information to be provided when it is available, which may have no relevance whatsoever to the design process. It is a particular problem with traditional Design and Build, which invariably demands the specification of door knobs at the same time as the spatial arrangement of the facility.

A number of respondents were concerned that the briefing is frequently a key issue but may not be given the appropriate resources or the appropriate 'Briefing Officer'. These Employer respondents pointed out that the persons responsible for briefing often have unrealistic expectations about the balance of cost, time and quality. Many were also concerned that the design team does not contribute to the brief, a gap often exacerbated by Employers looking for 'free advice'. Lack of strategy and inappropriately skilled Employer project leaders simply compound the problem.

The basis upon which the content of this information flow is built has an impact on the form and the effectiveness of the process. Research by others (Mackinder and Marvin 1982, p. 1) shows that early development stages of new projects develop quickly using just experience and the information contained in the Client's brief. It has been suggested by a number of sources that Consultants depend almost exclusively upon their own experience, and only in extreme cases do they undertake research or seek out written references.

This is partly accounted for by concerns over the commercial agenda: it has been noted in recent surveys (Garvin 1988, p. 43; Office of Science and Technology 1995, p. 9) that financial resources significantly restrict the time dedicated to a given project. The frequent complaint, that the 'bottom line' is the driver rather than quality, has been laboured previously. Certainly, the emphasis on finance in the Employers' comments confirmed this as a high priority and potentially high-risk area for most.

It was frequently observed that the 'level playing field' beloved by many in the construction industry has meant that price is often left as the main criterion for selection, and there remains little incentive for teams to add value. Competitive fee tendering has been detrimental to the development of the brief and encouraged premature design. It has led to a conflict where the Client is looking for extensive design development time but the Consultant is wishing to proceed to maximise cash flow. The trick is to achieve techniques that combine appropriate quality with good value and the essential timescale.

Figure 5.18 compares a model of common practice with the 'ideal'. Failure to maximise available knowledge sources contributes to the frequently quoted problem of 'lack of resource'. Few respondents applied any meaningful form of post-occupancy evaluation, and failed therefore to approach the potential of the 'ideal practice'. Although the Egan report looks primarily at the construction industry in the wider sense, it concurs that low profit margins within the industry conspire against appropriate research, training and ultimately efficiency.

Consultants also often depend on experience because they believe that the brief has been specified more objectively than may be the case. Responses indicate that Employers similarly use experience predominantly as the basis of brief specification. They do carry out a low-level of objective analysis and they do consider genuine organisation-led demand, albeit normally to a short time horizon. It is clear, however, that Consultants believe the use of objective analysis and organisation-led demand by their Employer is more widespread and of

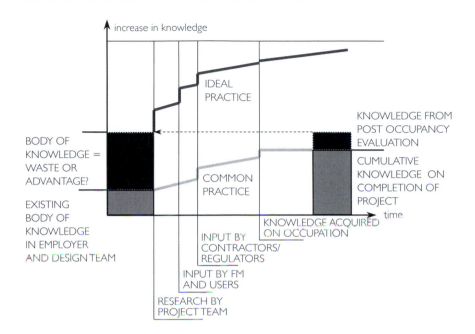

Figure 5.18 Potential for growth of project knowledge

greater depth. As a consequence there is little questioning of information or instructions.

Employers involved with simple repetitive projects believed that experience was a reasonable way of proceeding, while others felt that experience, being naturally retrospective, was not a good basis for developing future facilities. With one exception, there was little evidence that the future, or futures, are considered to any great extent. The problems besetting most Employers, and especially the stressed Employer's representative, are generally immediate. The lack of strategy that accompanies many decisions does not encourage the consideration of even a single future, let alone a range. Strategy, innovation, objective analysis and research are all interlinked. It is not proposed that 'experience' is devalued, but merely that it is appropriately supported.

Teams

The 1998 study demonstrates current practice, within the population, in terms of project team leadership and composition. As noted previously, there is a discrepancy between the views of Employers and Consultants as to which stage they are employed at. This may to some extent explain the difference in view as to their involvement with the development of the brief. It also reflects the finding of several other sources that projects are commenced with an uncertain idea by the Employer, and may then be developed for a significant period of time, before emerging as 'real projects', requiring the assembly of the team.

This was very much the view supported by several questionnaire respondents and interviewees. The Employers' response, noting that generally Consultants are appointed when there is 'a quantified requirement ... with a draft budget', is significant. Consultants consider that they are working in a more flexible environment, which is often not the true situation. A small number of interviewees, when questioned about 'secret knowledge', specifically referred to their common inability to 'show their hands' in terms of known budgets at the outset. This deliberate strategy is based either on reasons of commercial confidence or in the hope of achieving greater value per pound. Both motives would appear to be a flawed basis on which to proceed.

As methods of reducing risk, a significant number of Employers are actively adopting strategies that include:

• the employment of a professional in-house Client representative;
• the repetitive use of Consultants.

These strategies are seen to allow a two-way understanding and a learning process to develop. We are seeing the continuation of 'traditional' ideas, that more recently have been repackaged as 'Partnering' or 'Prime Contracting'. The openness and motivation of the new concepts may not be visible, but the ideal of 'continuity' is acknowledged widely by many Employers.

The appointment of an Architect as the first member of the external consultancy team is the majority experience of both Consultants and Employers. This is contrary to the views put forward by the RIBA strategic study and other sources. Public sector interviewees noted that they frequently worked to recognised procurement routes, and it was natural and traditional for them to appoint an Architect first. It was noted by some respondents that the alternative appointment of a Project Manager was simply a convenience, and effectively a substitute for their own in-house resources. Although Developers also noted they appointed Architects first they also clearly indicated that the Project Manager would lead the team. Concern about risks associated with finance and timescale in respect of Developer Employers, as referenced previously, would appear to lead the Developers' preference to use Project Managers as leaders of the project team, leaving Architects to be design team leaders/co-ordinators. User type clients (by a small percentage only) use Architects as project team leaders, influenced by the public sector view referred to above.

This very much endorses the popular stereotype of Consultants and Employers. The primary concerns about time and cost are addressed by the Project Manager, who is stereotypically viewed as having improved expertise in these fields. Employers with a high level of interest in Users and subsequent managers show their preference to employ Architects in the first instance, reflecting their stereo-typed image of potentially having a greater grasp of softer issues.

The question of leadership has received significant attention, and there is much debate as to which profession or professions should be leading a project team. A number of interviewees and questionnaire respondents noted that the relevant team leader was subject to the nature of the project and indeed the stage of the project. They felt that there was no particular profession for which this role is reserved. This endorses the view of people such as Fiedler and Bavelas (Davenport 1994, p. 230) who have proposed the model of the 'wheel of dominance'.

The idea of the 'one stop shop' now means that any profession may be found in a lead role. Other respondents also observed that the increased criticality of planning and engineering now means that these professions often lead the process. All Consultants tended to argue for leadership by their own profession, and all probably have a legitimate claim for *part* of the process.

The concept of changing project leaders would seem to have some relevance to current practice, and is encouraged by the increasing trend for 'one stop' and broad Consultancy services being offered by a consortium of specialist Consultants. It demands unity of purpose and agenda. The relevance of motivation is discussed in due course.

The 'debate' between individual traditional professions regarding their role within their team, specifically in relation to leadership, misses the point. Employers would be well advised to ignore the stereotyped images of any one particular profession, as there would appear to be no specific correlation between the level of failure and the profession of the team leader. Employers are advised to consider the personal skills and culture of the prospective candidates for the role, as opposed to the generic profession to which they purport to belong.

The Employer's project team is clearly very much subject to the form of the organisation and level of expertise contained within it. Survey data produced in 1989 (Franks 1998, p. 45) noted that 54 per cent of Employers have someone capable as acting as an internal Project Manager. However, one respondent notes that their company policy is to avoid employing anybody who does not contribute to their core business. Such a scenario will require a dramatically different approach to that taken by Employers with in–house professionals. As previously noted, the inexperienced Client may consider the project for a longer period before involving external Consultants, but then ultimately depend upon them to a greater extent. The range of Employer 'representative' is inevitably wide.

Nevertheless, the choice of leaders for the Employers' project teams reveals few surprises. As expected with a population comprising of a majority of experienced Clients, estates managers and development managers are the most common leaders. Within the Developer sector, MDs and directors remain in charge of the project team; this reflects the power-based organisational structure of most Developers, and particularly the middle sector that was heavily represented in this survey.

Curiously, facility managers show as occasional team leaders for user type Employers, which is in contrast to the rarity reported by Design and Build Contractors and Consultants. The projects covered by this report, however, include refurbishment and reconfiguration in addition to new build. Based upon the level at which facility management is used within the organisations interviewed, it is suggested that leadership by FM at briefing stage is generally restricted to minor projects in occupation.

Motivation as an issue was raised in relation to financial incentive for project

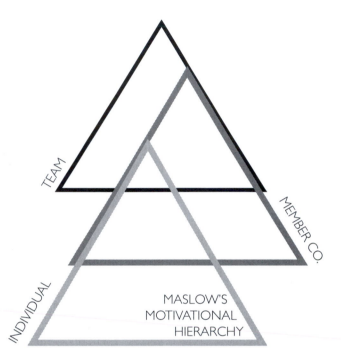

Figure 5.19 Nest of motivators

team organisations, but only one respondent referred specifically to the individual. Elsewhere, however, reference was made to the importance of the individual to the success of a project, particularly with regard to relationships. Without unity of purpose and motivation for all elements of the team, it would appear that the 'storming and norming' part of the process may not materialise. Maslow's motivational pyramid needs to be seen as a multiple and hierarchical 'nest', to provide for the needs of team, member company and individual. Figure 5.19 illustrates the concept, which requires the identification of appropriate motivators for both organisations and individuals within the team. The use of 'retention' to encourage continued performance, referred to by a number of respondents, has primary relevance to member companies. Alternative motivators for individuals require consideration. Project team leadership frequently focuses on 'deliverables', but style has enormous significance in relation to motivation and ultimate performance, of both individual and the team.

The Egan report is very much like a tug tethered to the front of an oil tanker. A range of initiatives and responses are currently being tested but, much like the tug and the oil tanker, it will take some time for the construction industry as a whole to turn and face a new direction. It is incumbent upon every Consultant and Employer to pull a little, and as a consequence, contribute towards the closing of the performance gap.

Concluding themes

From the main study 14 concluding themes can be drawn. They are summarised below under five sub-headings:

Failure levels

- Failure levels between expectation and realisation accord with previous surveys and literature, typically in excess of 10 per cent. The issues of function, finance and time are equally rated.
- Of Employer groups experiencing failure rates of over 35 per cent, Design and Build Contractors are proportionally high, and inexperienced Clients are proportionally low.
- Overall satisfaction with aesthetics is 'good' within all sectors, but remains a low profile issue.

Causation

- Generic areas of failing relate primarily to failure to meet finance and timescale target. Equally high is 'needs changed during project' which, it is suggested, is a euphemism for insufficiently developed user requirements.
- Opinions as to causation of failure agree on 'third party' issues related to planning authorities and contractors. Consultants, however, cite lack of sufficient and appropriate resource allocated by the Employer to briefing – no consensus with the Employer.

Agenda

- General view that the commercial agenda restricts appropriate input by Consultants into development.
- Mistrust in the private sector – hidden agendas and fear of collusion.

Briefing techniques

- Evidence that despite high 'user' involvement in the 'user Employer' sector, there remains a realisation gap for the user in areas of function and aesthetics – involvement is not enough.
- A variety of media are used for briefing, with targets for hard issues such as finance and timescale, but extensive use of wish lists and verbal meetings is common. Meetings with facility management are rare.
- Employers base briefing upon 'experience'. Consultants design similarly, but believe that the Employers' brief is based upon a higher level of objective and demand-led strategic analysis.

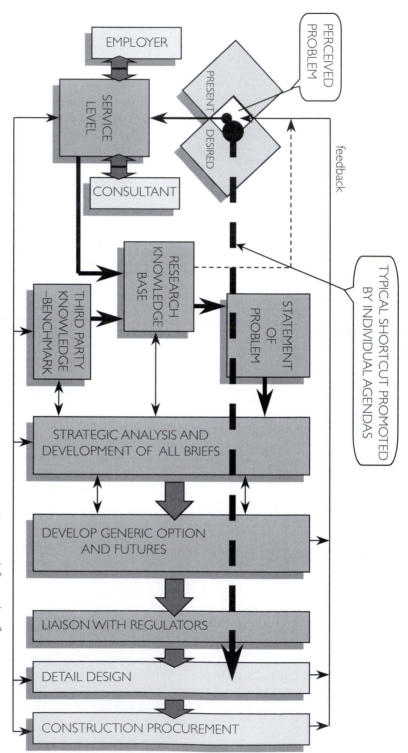

Figure 5.20 Briefing and design process shortcut

EMPLOYER

SERVICE LEVEL

CONSULTANT

PERCEIVED PROBLEM

PRESENT

DESIRED

feedback

TYPICAL SHORTCUT PROMOTED BY INDIVIDUAL AGENDAS

RESEARCH KNOWLEDGE BASE

THIRD PARTY KNOWLEDGE –BENCHMARK

STATEMENT OF PROBLEM

STRATEGIC ANALYSIS AND DEVELOPMENT OF ALL BRIEFS

DEVELOP GENERIC OPTION AND FUTURES

LIAISON WITH REGULATORS

DETAIL DESIGN

CONSTRUCTION PROCUREMENT

two-way information flow

Team structure

- Architects remain the preferred project team leader for user Employers, whereas project managers are favoured by Developers, but 62–9 per cent of all groups of Employers commission an Architect before other Consultants.
- Consultants believe that they are involved earlier in the project process than is Employers' perception.
- There remains a low perception of facility management within a Client's internal project team, despite a growing appreciation of their potential contribution and guilt at their exclusion.
- Design and Build Contractors would appear to lack appreciation of their roles as Employers in relation to external Consultants.

These themes form a basis of further exploration with respondents and analysis in the following chapters. Extended interviews, summarised in the next chapter, reveal levels of preconception and 'positioning' that perpetuates a number of concluding themes described above. A series of short case studies demonstrates that the simplest issues continue to dominate projects and lead to a performance gap and perceived failure. The idealised model of a typical project represented by Figure 5.20 is rarely evident.

The model includes for the identification of the problem, agreement of service levels, an appropriate basis for the briefing process and feedback. Unfortunately, it includes a shortcut that will be clearly recognisable to many readers, as it was to many contributors. This common shortcut to the process, together with a lack of feedback loops, is promoted by a variety of agendas and sources, and contributes to many of the above themes identified by respondents. Avoidance of the shortcut must be a key aim.

Much of the above falls clearly into the realms of communication in the broadest sense, and in particular the *quality* of communication. The following chapters discuss the above themes and model, in the context of current and future practice development.

6 Perceptions of current practice

Introduction

The objective results of the Author's study, gleaned by structured survey, were supported by a range of interviews, in addition to the frank and free open comment contained within the survey returns. It is considered that study of the patterns evolving from interviews and the open comment provide a valuable insight into real current practice, as opposed to what may be considered 'best practice'. This chapter reveals these key issues and extends the survey data by tackling issues of motive and preconception beyond the 'corporate policy'. There is no attempt to analyse objectively the interview comment. It is the flavour, colour and personal opinions that reveal the underlying truths of practice today.

Current practice in the 1990s has seen the development of a plethora of 'alternative' procurement and working methodologies. It would appear that, although certain proposals have commendable elements, in general there are no quantum steps forward from the traditional view of the briefing process and communication. The latter is clearly a key link between expectation and realisation. It is a fact, however, that many 'initiatives' remain focused on hard issues such as product, procurement system, reward and quality of workmanship. It is not suggested that these issues are of no importance, but that the softer issues of communication are worthy of equal attention.

Employers and Consultants alike are now subjected to an ever widening set of communication and procurement scenarios, with an ever increasing number of performance indicators and bench marking systems becoming available. Unless the primary causes of the performance gap described by the 1998 survey are addressed then all else is mere window dressing.

Towards the end of this chapter a number of case studies are included. They are briefly described scenarios with which many readers will be familiar. Their purpose is to identify the key failings and the lessons to be learnt. All are based on a combination of interviews and direct research of project documentation. Building on the data recorded in previous chapters, it was clear in many interviews, that although Consultants and Employers agreed on the reason for failure, there remained a gap between their perception of basic causes. 'Blame culture' is still rife.

The views of everyday practice

Interview framework and respondents

Seven formal interviews using a semi-structured agenda were undertaken with the following organisations:

1   a government department with a major estate and public interface;
2   a government department with responsibility for overseeing procurement by a large number of funded institutions;
3   a major privately owned FM and PM consultancy national and international;
4   local authority specialist division;
5   an international manufacturing and sales corporation;
6   a borough council procurement division;
7   a regional housing association.

Additionally, less formalised meetings were undertaken with a further seven organisations as follows:

i   regional division of a national contractor with D and B as a defined internal department;
ii   regional commercial developer;
iii   national private manufacturing company;
iv   property and development division of merchant bank;
v   regional division of a international contractor with D and B as a defined internal department;
vi   regional division of a national contractor;
vii   multi-national retailer.

The status and type of the organisation determined, to a large extent, the critical-ity of certain issues, and the way in which construction work was procured. Public sector organisations, for example, had great concern regarding budgets and often had prescriptive procedures in relation to their procurement methods. By com-parison, private sector organisations have a wider breadth of options available. This obviously reinforces the traditional stereotype divide between the sectors. It will be seen in subsequent chapters, however, that it is the public sector that is now beginning to lead the way forward in terms of innovation and the head-on tackling of the performance gap.

The formal interviews and, where possible, informal meetings followed six key headings, as a framework that reflected the response pattern perceived and returned in the questionnaires. Figure 6.1 maps the interview topics and their inter-relationship. The interviews sought to relate particular respondents' own questionnaire responses to the general patterns, and explore the reasoning behind their particular response. The key issues arising from the interviews are described below, grouping together like responses as appropriate, following the framework of the interview agenda.

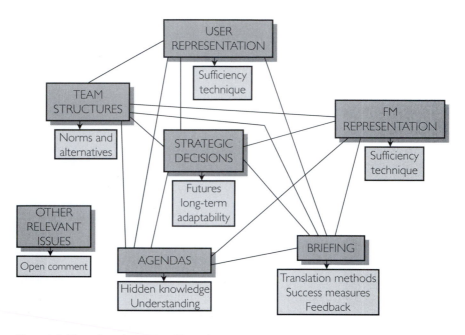

Figure 6.1 Map of semi-structured interviews

External consultant team and team leaders

There was a unanimous agreement by the four public sector bodies interviewed that the traditional procurement route starting with the appointment of an Architect is 'normal'. Within the public sector, expectation of the Architect is high and the management and co-ordination role expected is significant. There is a belief that project management is a role that they prefer to be undertaken by the Architect, or alternatively is a role that they feel they undertake themselves. It was true that public sector respondents had professional staff capable of the role, but clearly internal pressures and agendas often prevent objective and appropriate project management.

Other interviewees saw project managers merely as a 'convenience' rather than a separate discipline. The most cynical felt that project managers brought little to the table. It is clear from Consultants that the role of project manager ranges from real management of a project down to merely chairman of meetings and recorder of minutes. Referring back to the study described in Chapter 4 (Somogyi 1997), many Employers saw PM as a purely administrative function, as opposed to any form of real or dynamic management. This view will clearly raise a few hackles. In fairness to project managers it needs to be observed that the management ability of architectural profession is equally patchy. From discussions with public sector Clients, however, there is no grass roots evidence that this particular profession is as incompetent as suggested by the RIBA strategic studies some years ago. It may be that the harsh criticism contained in these studies has in fact had a beneficial effect on some members of the profession.

Problems related to the issues of role, however, were identified; it was noted that many Client bodies rarely produce an appropriate service brief for the actual consultancy services, and therefore Consultants start work with very unclear roles. It was felt that although there may be high expectations of consultant services, it was frequently the case that there was a disparity between the service expected and service offered, simply through lack of communication.

Very clearly, the private sector has a much broader approach to the issue of consultancy and management of projects. Two multinational companies use project managers on most projects to provide the single package of deliverables that incorporates whatever design disciplines are required. Both the companies made it clear that they focus upon their own business and to quote: 'We only want to employ people that can make our *widgets*'. The view was expressed that construction professionals employed *within* a manufacturing industry have insufficient opportunity to achieve full potential, due to the repetitive nature of their experiences, and by implication external Consultants bring more to the project.

This issue was raised by several experienced Employers in relation to the merits or otherwise of in-house professionals or third parties. Although by no means unanimous, the general consensus was that the employment of external Consultants had benefits. It was somewhat discouraging to learn however that these benefits were primarily seen as commercial: the opportunity to 'turn on the tap' when needed and the ability to extract 'free' initial services.

Several experienced Employers confessed that they are still experimenting with alternative procurement methods, currently oscillating between the traditional Architect/JCT 80 form and Design and Build processes. Neither processes were fulfilling Clients' expectations. It was clear that both routes started from the same line. The basic building blocks, namely method of briefing, team structure and interpretation methodology, are common to both procurement strategies. The way that the 'blocks' are built is of little value if the 'blocks' themselves are inappropriate.

The expectation of other private sector Employers, within the experienced category, noted that teams were formed according to the primary disciplines involved. It was expected that team leaders would vary as jobs developed from planning through to design and onto construction. The Employers expressing this view seemed unaware of the high level of innovation that it contained. It was suggested in the Latham report that, in effect, this should happen as those involved with feasibility give way to those involved with detail design and construction. It is not evident from these Employers however, that they set out any system or structure to enable this scenario to occur. Nevertheless, all who observed its occurrence, encouraged it, and facilitated its continuation. The cultural issues involved are significant, and experience has shown that within the consultancy world, concept designers maintain involvement often beyond their remit and into the detail design stage. Similarly, detail designers frequently involve themselves in aspects of procurement and tendering, but again are acting beyond their defined role. It is, in part, human nature; it is also, in part, failure to appreciate the value of others in the supply chain.

Design and Build Contractors generally have in-house design co-ordinators, but nevertheless expect Architects to take on the role of design team leader and co-ordinator. The range of leadership and team structure scenarios clearly influence project success. Appropriate motivation and clarity of role are seen to be critical as a sound foundation, but rarely noted in practice.

The confusion of roles evident in survey responses was endorsed by interview. Clarity of role is one issue that is certainly not readily apparent in many Design and Build contracts. It is true that the relationship between Design and Build Contractors, as Employers, and their Consultants does vary and the expectations from both sides will adapt accordingly. But the duplicity of in-house D and B co-ordinators, and Architects as design team co-ordinators, often leads to dissatisfaction on both parts. The 'link of convenience', shown in Figure 5.7, was evident between the Design and Build Contractor's *Employer* and the Design and Build Contractor's *Consultant*. It only serves to confuse the issue. There has been much criticism of Consultant's lack of enthusiasm for the Design and Build procurement route, and it has been suggested that this is frequently due to cultural issues attributed to Consultants. Undoubtedly, problems of cultural fit will be evident from both Consultant and Design and Build Contractor, but it appears that issues of role and motivation are fundamental. Much more care is needed to promote more widespread and clear understanding of roles and responsibilities within this procurement scenario.

Facility management

The questionnaires overall, show an under-representation by Facility Management. The reasons for this response became clear. There is a great deal of misinformation and misunderstanding as to the role. For example, one public sector housing organisation initially believed that they were dealing with FM as a purely operational maintenance-type exercise. On further discussion, however, it was clear that some strategic Facility Management and design was indeed taking place and informing new developments. A particular scheme currently ongoing was considering a variety of potential futures. The scheme was designed to incorporate the future conversion of roof space to provide carers' accommodation, as the first tenants become older and potentially in need of 24-hour care. Similarly, this elderly persons' development has installed substantial IT and data systems to cater for the high level of anticipated computer literacy of older people in the future. Separately, the organisation was using adaptable design strategies on another scheme to allow for changing accommodation needs over the life of the building shell. This is probably one of the most active examples of real strategic Facility Management seen in the 1998 survey, and it was happening almost as a by-product of good practice.

Other Public Sector organisations deal with Facility Management at a low level, but all expressed concern that they were not considering longer term issues or the strategic issues of Facility Management and environment. Respondents noted that there was a deficiency of space and facility data and this encouraged the low profile of FM. This would appear to be very much a case of 'chicken and egg'. In terms of an FM input into briefing and design, most public sector organisations felt that there was a significant role, but appreciation of the advantages was embryonic. It was noted that there was a role within PFI for a Facility Management role at a strategic briefing level, but there was some dismay that external FM Consultants had not taken any great initiative in this field, and that many PFI submissions are dominated by the financier or contractor. Personal experience supports the view that at a design level, FM rarely has any involvement.

The multinational Employers noted that where any strategic Facility Management skills were required in terms of space planning, life cycle analysis or IT systems for example, then specialist projects were enabled that involved the appointment of specialists for this one-off 'problem'. Within the private sector, there remains a dependence upon traditional design teams to consider strategic facility issues, such as adaptability, life cycle and reinvestment issues related to the fabric. One respondent notes that although they are concerned with a long-term facility as an investment, it must 'look after itself' while they get on with their business. This 'head in the sand' attitude is becoming less common, but Consultants must realise that to many businesses, the building is either a small part of their overall investment, or simply a necessary evil.

Within the Developer and Design and Build sectors, Facility Management appears to have virtually no profile. The demands of 12-year tenant/funding warranties imposed upon Developers means that there is a limited interest in the facilities' long-term future. Developments held as investment, of course represent a different case. A single Design and Build Contractor considered Facility Management to have a significance, predominately due to their involvement in the PFI arena, where they consider life cycle analysis to be a critical element.

Within the private sector user Employer arena, internal Facility Management clearly remains at an operational level. This is not intended to denigrate operational FM, which has the potential to maximise the utility value of any facility and to optimise support to the business. It is, however, somewhat akin to 'shutting the stable door'. Strategic input can offer future potential for a facility, and as a consequence enable future operational FM to be more productive. It is worthy of note, however, that even in such situations where FM is given a greater profile, it is predominantly in respect of the commercial agenda. Emphasis is placed upon future costs of facilities in so far as finishes, fittings and fabric are concerned. There is little evidence in everyday practice of adaptability or flexibility for a variety of futures being considered. It clearly shows failure to understand the role that Facility Management can offer in support of the 'traditional' Consultant.

Users

Many organisations, whether private or public sector, are providing facilities for a tenant or another department. To this extent, they do not consider the *ultimate* user because they presume that 'others' will have considered the final users requirements. Developers and Design and Build contractors see the 'user' very much in the form of the person on whose behalf they are providing a facility, and this is generally an organisation. It is also clear that in many of these situations the prospective purchaser or tenant will have provided a highly prescriptive brief, detailed in nature, and often providing little design scope.

Developers are often required to satisfy demands of the long-term investor, either a bank or pension fund. Their input into the brief is generally to ensure that there is no deleterious material and that the building is capable (based upon retrospective experience) of performing in accordance with the investment appraisal. Perversely, it is also noted by some Design and Build Contractors that government departments and other public sector organisations frequently produce specifications that demand completely unachievable periods to first maintenance. Again, this points to a lack of FM involvement and an over-prescriptive and unrealistic performance brief. More emphasis on real requirements and a provision for value engineering cost analysis within the design process would appear much more beneficial.

In accordance with TQM and overall business philosophy, the multinational manufacturer involves users in the form of staff at all levels of a project, whereas other private manufacturers with a heavier power base were seen to follow a less open briefing procedure.

It is depressing for anyone involved with a project to find on completion that some section of the user body is unhappy with their sparkling new facility. Respondents provided numerous examples, the following being typical.

Example 1 The facility was refurbished in part. New flooring was installed to the satisfaction of the briefing officer and most of the users, except for the cleaning staff who had not been consulted. On completion the Employer was obliged to purchase alternative cleaning equipment just for the refurbished area, which represented only a minor proportion of the whole facility, but demanded a specific and unique cleaning regime.

Example 2 Significant care was taken to design a major reception desk in a hospital. The design was based carefully around the space requirements for document trolleys and personnel. Administrative porters were not consulted. A simple consultation would have revealed that bulk documents, delivered out of hours, used much larger trolleys. The new 'improved' design now required double man handling of documentation.

Where users involve members of the public that have choice, such as in the situation of retailers and leisure facility providers, then the organisations note they have good procedures to ascertain customer satisfaction and feedback. Similarly, other organisations within the public sector and within facility consultancy are very conscious of the need to consult with end users and have procedures in place, but clearly there is a difficulty in managing this process. It is believed generally that user involvement can 'wind up cost' and can adjust or expand various agendas.

Most organisations attempt to control this process by proposing an internal co-ordinator to act as a funnel/translator. It is accepted by a number of organisations that this becomes a critical role if users' requirements are to be accurately reflected through to the design team. There is general concern that where user departments are permitted to brief external Consultants directly, the potential for major disaster is high. An example is given of a college project £1M over budget, and one year late because the employing department thought that the contract included the fit-out – it did not!

The briefing process

Within the public sector, the briefing process tends to evolve almost universally through a series of written documents which the project co-ordinators attempt to have 'signed off' at each stage. With the exception of Design and Build contractors and Developers' who tend to be dealing with professional to professional, the interface between the lay Client body/user and professional is the critical element. One public sector housing authority, noted the example where, despite numerous meetings, production of drawings and Architects impressions, the lay user party failed to realise the fundamental indication of the layout involving traffic movements. Failure was acknowledged to lie with the internal project sponsor for simply not appreciating the issue and ensuring appropriate communication.

The generous acceptance of this problem by the Employer does not negate, however, the necessity of all involved in any project to ensure that the other party understands. Failure should not be excused by reference to minutes, drawing issue sheets, briefing documents and so on. It is a Consultant's duty to ensure understanding and not simply to provide information.

It is also noted by more than one public sector organisation that users tend not to think of the future and are occupied by immediate problems. Again in this situation, it must be responsibility of the Consultant to offer the broader view. The failure to expose the implications of instant (and often expedient) solutions tends to be a common route to medium/long term dissatisfaction. Short-term gain and long-term pain for both Employer and Consultant is commonplace.

Experience as the basis for providing briefing information is evidenced by the questionnaires. Virtually all the interviewees considered that experience was a very important element of providing a brief, but most considered that this must be coupled with a strong strategic view of the future. The structured survey, however, showed real strategy to be rare. One particular interviewee who extolled the virtues of the strategic brief was known personally by the Author to produce room data sheets, before the size and form of the building was established!

A lone manufacturer noted that in projects that were non-repetitive nature, they used a zero-base approach to development of the brief. Facility Consultants supported zero base as a starting point. Too frequently, they noted, the production of room data sheets by users are simply based upon existing accommodation plus 5 per cent 'because they deserve it'. Developer and retail respondents consider demographics and financial return in depth, but due to inevitable repetition in the building types, experience in terms of the brief and production of a standard specification is commonplace, and probably appropriate.

The multinational manufacturer, by virtue of company philosophy, takes a real strategic and demand-based view of any project. Briefs are intentionally broad and are often instigated from another continent. A typical hypothetical brief to the UK operation for example may be 'absorb the French IT division into the UK centre'. This global view then requires transformation to a locally achievable goal.

This was one of the few examples of phased briefing. It allowed for the consideration of design in such a way that each layer of brief and design could be considered as independent strategies, and evaluated accordingly against the brief without the baggage of premature, and potentially conflicting, information.

Agendas

The issue of secret knowledge and agendas is believed by the public sector to be insignificant. It is accepted that user groups always attempt to 'empire build' and, as one respondent notes, 'user satisfaction focuses on the wallpaper'. But generally, they believe that the Consultancy/construction industry is open. This sector takes solace from the formal auditing system which is universal.

By contrast, private sector user Clients and Developers are less comfortable. There are concerns regarding 'commercial brinkmanship' and secrecy which can result in Consultants and Contractors colluding to close ranks. Failure rates noted by the interview respondents range from the very low to 60 per cent or more in terms of time and cost for one organisation. What was unclear and could not be explained by any Employer was the possible motive that Consultants might have in maintaining bodies of secret knowledge. It is believed to be a myth. The Consultant is selling time and expertise to a variety of Employers. Simplistically, it is a balance of resources against the Employers' timescale. The 'conspiracy' in reality has little basis.

Issues of quality, finance and timescale are described by all respondents. However, the motive behind concerns about finance and timescale appear to vary between private and public sector. The example of one multinational organisation notes that currently delays on a £15M building mean that they are having to store £100M worth of machinery in another country and delay the onset of production. Other examples in the retail sector relate to the absolute nature of completion times by virtue of TV advertising programmes and staff recruitment programmes, that are initiated before the building is even started. Depressingly, some Employers do not believe that any projects complete on time and on cost, if compared with the original briefing and cost plan.

Public sector concerns are less in relation to timescale. Traditionally cost has been structured around the financial year and governmental funding. 'Life cost' was less critical than adherence to the funding structure. It was noted however that with alternative procurement strategies and private investment increasing, sensitivity to total cost issues is rising.

To some extent, time and cost agendas within the public and private sectors reinforce the stereotype of the organisations. But it is very clear that this gap is closing fast. 'Best' practice public sector and private sector, in terms of aspiration and achievement, are inseparable.

Concluding issues

The interviews serve to demonstrate the real views of everyday practice and there was found to be a significant correlation between the different types of organisations interviewed. The general outcome of open comment within interviews is summarised by Figure 6.2 and the following bullet points.

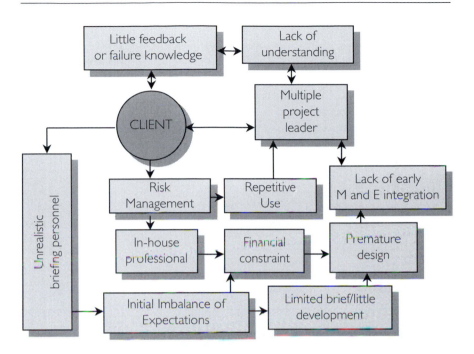

Figure 6.2 Key areas of open comment

- Commonly, Employers' response to risk management is the use of in-house professionals or the repetitive use of external Consultants.
- Frequently there is a lack of compatibility between the standards and tolerances within the building industry and the Employers' own industry.
- Employers accept that briefing personnel are often unrealistic, and there is an inherent imbalance of expectations due either to financial constraints or to failure to develop the brief appropriately.
- Poorly developed brief and inappropriate financial restraints frequently lead to premature design, in which lack of M and E integration is a clear element.
- Compulsory competitive tendering, particularly within the public sector, was not felt to be providing the best value for money – because of a lack of design development.
- Employers felt that the concept of multiple project leaders to maximise expertise to each part of the project was of benefit.
- The majority of Employers believe that they have little true understanding of their failures and insufficient feedback. Post-occupation evaluations and feedback to design teams are rare.

It can be seen from preceding sections that there remains a high proportion of what one would consider a traditional linear response to the formation of project teams and the communication of expectations.

Although there is some encouragement that issues such as facility management are receiving 'air time', it was depressing to have the main survey data graphically confirmed in relation to the briefing process itself. It may well be that the process is in the ownership of the Employer, but it is nevertheless incumbent upon all involved to move this key element forward for mutual benefit. The room data sheet based upon 'existing plus 5 per cent' should not be tolerated by any member of the project team.

The study revealed a vast number of anecdotal stories by both Consultants and Employers used to demonstrate specific concerns of the respondents. A small number of these have been pursued to ensure factual accuracy, and there follow nine brief case studies demonstrating typical problems in practice of which most readers will be familiar. The simplicity of the problem in each case is clear, but the industry continues to make the same mistake far too often. They are worthy as reminders of the everyday consequences of complacency, and of the use of traditional linear processes.

Case studies

Design and Build multistorey residential development

A graphic case of the ill-defined role of Employer and Consultant is shown in a significant central London residential project, which was procured on a Design and Build basis. The case embodies many of the elements that lead to anomalies within the Design and Build contractor responses, and it fully supports some of Egan's key criticisms of the industry.

Problems were encountered by both the Design and Build Contractor, the Consultants and the Employer in terms of interpretation of requirements, cost, and time. The following represent the key issues that arose as a consequence.

Inadequate and inappropriate brief The Employer provided a highly prescriptive brief involving a significant amount of general and detailed CAD drawings; it was also supported by an extensive written specification. The Design and Build Contractor accepted the brief at face value believing it to represent an appropriately designed scheme, and to be consistent with the written Employer's requirement and the presented design. External consultants were appointed by the Design and Build contractor on this basis. Fortunately it was quickly proven that, despite outward appearances, the design was unworkable since it did not fit the site and was unbuildable.

Communication and control Contracts having been completed, the Contractor's response to resolve the countless inconsistencies was to demand that their Consultants liaise directly with the ultimate Employer, with little control being exerted regarding the management of this interface.

Costs The Consultants were appointed on a competitive fee bid but with a changing goal and role. Cost soared and antagonism prevailed. Similarly, the Contractor was subject to a fixed price but found the product was not equally fixed and therefore embarked upon an extensive 'value engineering exercise' that involved the design of multiple options and tendering packages for individual elements.

Lesson

The project demonstrates lack of profit as a barrier to motivation. It also clearly reinforces survey results, noting the essential nature of the appropriate brief and the need for appropriate management of the interface between Client and design team. The delegation of the Employer's (the D and B Contractor) role by allowing Consultants to deal directly with the ultimate Employer was inappropriate, and demonstrated a disregard of the Design and Build procurement route.

Leisure pool refurbishment

The project consisted of the rebuilding and extension of a significant leisure pool and associated facilities. The Employer was part of the public sector and the works were procured through a traditional route. Problems encountered included a significant contract overrun and poor quality on site. Although this book does not attempt to deal with issues of Contractors' workmanship, decisions taken during briefing and design development were influential in creating on-site problems. Issues that are pertinent included the following.

Project Brief A simple brief forming a mere three sides of A4 text required that many decisions be made by the Consultant team. The brief itself, despite its small size, was a traditional closed loop statement offering little opportunity for phased consideration of information, or for evaluating issues. The Consultant's service brief was similarly restricted and followed standard RIBA appointment in respect of the Architect, who was then tasked with writing service briefs for other Consultants.

Contract Contract documentation and procurement route provided for a closed prescriptive definition of the works to be undertaken. The reality of substantial refurbishment inevitably uncovered hidden issues to which the contract scenario was unable to respond satisfactorily.

Team Despite the appointment of M and E Consultants to design the M and E systems in detail, installation design remained part of the Contractors remit. Involvement of M and E contractors late in the process, due to the inevitable commercial agenda requiring retendering to subcontractors after the main Contractor had secured the contract, meant a very late involvement with significant problems of integration.

Timescale Management failures by all parties were evident in relation to programming, where compliance with the apparent critical path gave a false sense of security, and allowed many other issues to become critical.

Teams again Chemistry and culture became key issues as conflicts within the team escalated, and failure to agree on goals destroyed motivation.

Lesson

The project exposed a variety of issues that conspired to prevent the completion of a satisfactory project. Issues of culture and chemistry are not uncommon and can only be resolved by familiarity and understanding. It is an advertisement on behalf of 'partnering' as a way of ensuring that parties thrown together for a particular project, become a team as opposed to a collection of personal agendas.

Other problems essentially related to the perception of the project as a whole. The prescriptive brief and traditional fixed price fixed quantum contract, in retrospect, was inappropriate for a project that demanded a dynamic system capable of constant re-appraisal and adaptation to suit circumstances. An approach that allowed a shared financial motive for all involved to achieve the overall objectives of the Employer and within the Employer's time and cost budgets might have helped.

Member owned sports club

A small lottery funded project for a sports club included a simple brief: 'maximum improvement to facilities and minimum cost'. Several issues arose during the process.

The multi-headed Client The Client in this project was a committee with varying levels of expertise and understanding. Each member had their own desires and aspirations for the project. The design developed to encompass the primary brief and to allay comments by various factions of the Employer, with additional elements added somewhat randomly. As a consequence the tenders exceeded the budget, which had always varied somewhat, depending which member of the Client body one interviewed.

Costs Cost savings demanded a re-design. This was embarked upon with a unanimous brief that savings were to be made in finishes and fittings, with a maximum volume of building being retained.

Unreliability In view of cost restraints the Employer instructed the design team to proceed with minimal ground investigation. Consequently ground conditions were found to be variable and more difficult than expected, resulting in additional foundation costs and delay.

Lesson

The lessons learnt from this project relate to the need to manage multi-headed entities appropriately, the Client in this case, but potentially the design team in order to ensure a consistent, realistic and unanimous brief.

The second primary failure is that of communication, in the sense of promoting genuine understanding of the implication of change. In this case it demanded the removal of the 'wallpaper', so often associated with success-ful projects. Inadequate management of risk and expectation on this project led to a 'perceived' performance gap, despite the fact that the project actu-ally fulfilled the revised brief in terms of cost and accommodation.

A Prestigious business park

The issue of aesthetics has a curiously low weighting amongst Employers, but nevertheless it is clear that the ambivalence to this brief occurs only when appearance is satisfactory or good. Examples of projects being completed and then providing surprises to Employers, and warranting action, are uncommon.

One example in a prestigious business park is an exception. The build-ing was completed some 10 years ago, but within three years would receive major remedial treatment, purely for the purpose of improving appearance. How had such a high-profile building passed through a wide range of Employer appraisals, design team reviews, and of course the local planning authority without attracting attention? The key is again communication.

In this particular project it would appear that communication, in the sense of design presentation, both drawn and verbal provided 'rose tinted glasses'. Attractive presentation techniques, which were later not helped by subtle but significant cost saving changes to detail design, 'oversold' the scheme.

Lesson

The management of realising expectation demands appropriate and honest communication. The results of design in the construction industry are highly visible. It is essential that communication and media techniques are focused to provide open and true interpretation on behalf of all relevant parties. 'Artistic licence' may well quickly promote a scheme at the outset, but it is the finished product upon which success is judged.

Multinational distributor

It has been noted elsewhere that educational background and culture have a significant effect upon understanding. The example of a major distribution centre procured on behalf of a continental European organisation demonstrates the point. The brief was developed with a design team based upon strategic decisions and criteria proposed by the Employer and generated from experience gained in continental Europe.

One aspect of the project demanded an assessment of the level of control possible over suppliers, and the punctuality of UK drivers. Design proceeded, based upon the brief, but it was discovered after completion that much greater tolerance was required for the operation in the UK. Consequently, significant adjustments were made to lorry waiting areas. Fortunately in this case, land and resources were available.

Lesson

This demonstrates the point that experience, although important, and clearly from survey work the basis of most briefing, must be treated with caution. A significant strategic decision was made without the benefit of relevant data. In this instance the design team were not part of the strategic briefing team and simply accepted this particular element of the brief, which subsequently proved to be erroneous.

City-based and failing retail outlet

Strategic decision making requires future scenarios to be considered. Failure to consider such future implications of design was demonstrated by a significant retail development constructed in North London. It incorporated basement car parking with retail space above, accessed from the street and the car park. The design involved two sets of check-outs and security points. One served the street access and the other served the car park access. The retail unit failed partly because the overhead to maintain the duplicated security, and the losses encountered, were too great.

A strategic rethink of the development by another retailer demonstrated that by simple reconfiguration, the development could be simplified to provide much reduced operational costs. It also created customer visibility and a comfortable and desirable retail environment. This was completed and is now proving to be a highly successful retail location.

Lesson

The lesson to be learnt here relates to the original Client, representing the classic multi-headed Employer with a series of agendas. The facility and operational briefs, however, were insufficiently developed, resulting in a design which was doomed to failure before its conclusion. The design team for the original retail Employer had no strategic input. There was no strategic facility management thinking involved and, as a consequence, little consideration of operational futures.

Fire department training facility

A county fire service commissioned the design and construction of a training facility. Essentially the building consisted of a non-combustible house. Its primary function was the training of fire-fighters in simulated domestic fire conditions. The design included a sloping concrete floor to the upper storey with 100-millimetre drainage tubes through the external walls, for obvious reasons. Design works had been completed to a high level in conjunction with a range of users' representatives. The Design responsibility was transferred to the Contractor for detail design and construction.

The interpretation of the Employer's design included several 'howlers'. Fundamental errors included:

1   The floor sloping *away* from drainage tubes.
2   The installation of normal domestic 13 amp power outlets, and associated electrical installation.

The problems in translating the Employer's requirement and concept design into reality were overcome, but not without extensive cost by the Design and Build contractor and a significant time penalty to the Employer.

Lesson

Again, communication is the key failing in this project. It demonstrates how even an appropriate brief complete with an advanced design, may not be sufficient to ensure accurate translation of requirements to the ultimate design team. Issues of culture, educational background, minimal research and 'experience' all conspire to ensure a lack of understanding.

Post-Latham

The last 5 years has seen much debate within the construction industry, in the widest sense, aimed at improvement of quality, again in the widest sense. We have seen that current practice incorporates some innovation but continues to repeat, time after time, the same mistakes, encouraged by traditional linear thinking and systems. Most members of the construction industry are attempting to improve and are certainly aware of the debate for change. New initiatives are being tried, but clearly practices that have been commonplace for decades will not be overturned in an instant.

We will briefly consider the drivers of this change of opinion before seeking, in Chapter 7, to determine the effectiveness of initiatives designed to implement change.

Current thinking – not current practice!

The Latham report (1994) and its heir, the Construction Act 1997, received much anecdotal criticism (Duncan-Willis, *Building*, 21 November 1997, p. 22) and, according to Iain Duncan QC, the legislation was misconceived; however, briefing has become a focus of attention in the post-Latham era (Barrett 1995b, p. 7), with the Client at the core.

A common cause of complaint is that Clients are ill-prepared with an inadequate brief (Garvin 1988, p. 13). Latham proposed that they should undertake more extensive viability and feasibility testing using an external advisor if necessary, but not necessarily the design team leader or project manager, before deciding upon a procurement route. Clearly the level of research into the issue of briefing has been increasing in recent years. It should be of major concern, therefore, that briefing remains a simple mechanical exercise concentrating on physical delivery in the form of datasheets and checklists, and still misses the wider strategic implications and the 'how questions'.

Latham also proposed a greater emphasis on 'partnering' as a means of establishing long term teams with common goals and motivations. With respect to Consultants and Employers it would appear that this has long been accepted as informal practice, as shown by Huxley (Barrett 1995) in his 1993 research into the source of Consultants' work, which notes:

- 65 per cent of work is from existing Clients;
- 35 per cent of work is from new Clients, of which 61 per cent is via referrals.

Partnering in the Latham context, as a 'new' system of working, is more relevant to the construction part of the project cycle. The results of the University of Bath survey, published in late August 1998, however, show price-driven contracts to remain prevalent, with a strong resistance to 'partnering'. The principle has some way to go before it is common practice.

Some parties cynically consider 'partnering' to be a further opportunity for 'exploitation' of good will. Such an attitude is certainly evident in a number of partnering projects: although the partner's senior managers may be sincere in their aspirations, this often does not cascade throughout the project team.

Few individuals, let alone organisations, will undertake any action without a motive. Commercial motive is, however, not automatically a barrier to innovation. Gazeley Properties, for example, have been highly innovative and praised for their approach to partnering and supply chain management, but work closely to a commercial agenda. They note that they seek to 'maximise margin and satisfy client aspirations in terms of utility and cost'. Their early reconciliation of the needs of user and funder with those of their suppliers has required development of their own partnering techniques, but as Pat McGillycuddy is quoted (Cox and Townsend 1998, p. 181), he prefers this to be seen as 'a sustainable approach to optimising the supply chain'.

Quality has achieved a similarly high profile, but Garvin (1988, p. 5) also gives evidence to suggest that some UK buildings are over-specified and thus unnecessarily costly. On this basis a more critical definition of quality is demanded, considering balance, as referred to in Chapter 2. It is accepted that an over-emphasis of time in the context of the 'traditional' procurement route means that many construction projects suffer from poor definition due to inadequate time and thought at the early stage; there is often a sense of urgency fuelled by desire for an immediate solution (CIB 1997, p. 8).

Recent documentation and best practice guidance from sources such as The Construction Industry Board (1997, p. 7) and the Office of Science and Technology (1995, p. 31) have reiterated many of the concerns expressed by other sources, namely levels of Client dissatisfaction, lack of strategy, and failure to consider life costs and post-occupancy evaluation.

As the issues discussed by Latham became more 'topical' and accepted as part of practice in the 1990s, Professor Daniel Jones of Cardiff University proposed 'lean construction', along the lines of the systems used in car and Aerospace Industry (*Building*, 27 February 1998). Jones says:

> There is large scope for improvement. It is a flawed process because there is wide-spread attachment to the idea that every project is different, from the Architect through to the sub-contractor, but all buildings share similar processes.

Graves (*Building*, 27 February 1998) agrees, noting that due to poor design, poor logistics, poor purchasing and poor production, there is a reworking rate of 30 per cent. He notes that the construction industry spends more on litigation each year than it does on the research and development. Rose of Balfour Beatty has been working with Graves implementing the Bath University Agile Construction Initiative within his company, and reports a 40–50 per cent productivity increase and a 28 per cent cost saving (*Building*, 3 July 1998, p. 10).

A balance to the 'lean' standardised design and construction approach is embodied in Hilliers (*Building*, 21 November 1997) quote regarding the status of professions:

> True professions exist where the application of knowledge that is socially important, but involves risk, cannot be reduced to rules and procedures because cases are different.

Alistair McAlpine (*Building*, 14 August 1998, p. 22) offers support to this view in his response to the Egan report, supporting improvement but noting:

> Buildings are not like cars – every project is a prototype.

Thus the agenda for future practice debate is developing, with the potential for standardisation being high on the agenda.

The Egan report

The last major Government instigated design/construction report was published on 15 July 1998. The Egan report (*Rethinking Construction*) was the output from a government task force charged with the task of advising the government on the scope for improvement, efficiency and quality within the construction industry. The task force was chaired by Sir John Egan and included representatives from a range of major private Employers of the construction industry, together with some representation from public sector and academia. The conclusions of the report were built upon the basis of the Latham report and reflect many of the concepts and views put forward by other sources in Chapters 2, 3 and 4.

'Under achievement' and 'Client dissatisfaction' are considered to be rife; the industry is considered to be competitive on price only, and lacks 'quality'. The main aims set by the report can be summarised as follows:

1   year-on-year financial improvements consisting of 10 per cent cut in construc-
     tion costs, 10 per cent improvement in productivity, 10 per cent boost in
     profits and turnover;
2   greater integration of the design and construction processes;
3   increased standardisation of built forms;
4   improvements in timescale by the use of the 'lean production' techniques;
5   end of competitive tendering based on price evaluation only;
6   phasing out of formal contracts in favour of partnering arrangements.

The report has significant relevance to this book and the 1998 study, although it concentrates its efforts on the broader aspects of the construction industry. Commendable targets such as 20 per cent improvement in accidents and defects are noted, but fall outside of the context of this study. Particular issues relevant to this study concern the following:

1   failure to resource appropriately, in terms of fees and time, the design stage
     of a project;
2   the need for ongoing relationships with external Consultants and Contractors,
     for improvement of understanding and cultural compatibility;
3   the need for Clients to accept their responsibilities for effective design;
4   design to encompass whole life costs and sustainability.

The report has received significant criticism insofar as it concentrates on major projects. Concerns are also expressed that targets set may be achievable in the short term, but cannot be sustained year-on-year. It is further noted that the targets themselves are somewhat arbitrary. However, the report has received significant coverage in the press since its launch. It primarily reiterates good practice but contains little that has not been stated elsewhere, as referred to in previous sections of Chapters 2, 3 and 4. However, the primary aims, if not all of the means, must be commended.

The ideals of the report have unquestionably instigated a number of initiatives. Government agencies and divisions, such as the MoD, have embraced these ideas and are clearly being used as a medium to push forward improvements within the construction industry and, some might cynically say, political agendas. It has gone much further than this however. Although elements of the private sector have, at 'best' practice level, employed techniques to achieve real improvement for some years, they have tended to be major organisations, such as Slough Estates and Gazeley Properties. Recently, however, the inclusion of much smaller companies is giving credibility to Egan ideals, at a realistic and everyday level. The next chapter seeks to consider the variety of initiatives that are being used currently to bring forward Latham/Egan targets and ultimately close the gap between expectation and realisation.

7 Alternatives or hot air?

Introduction

The profile given to the issue of performance by the Egan report and its predecessor, the Latham report, is commendable. It is, however, dependent upon appropriate initiatives being developed. They must be capable of being implemented widely; equally they must also have the capability of producing tangible benefits for all involved.

Many of the criticisms levelled at the concepts in Egan related to the emphasis that was placed upon major Employers. It was good to see that a group of UK retailers have engaged Leeds University to consider improvements to the procurement of refurbishment in line with Egan ideals (Cook, *Building*, 26 November 1999, p. 13). Companies involved, such as Pizza Express and Boots (the chemist) are clearly significant Employers, but are generally involved with, what are, individually, considered 'minor' projects.

This chapter considers the progress and potential of strategies that are currently being explored, in relation to what has been described as being the causation of the performance gap. Are current strategies really tackling the basic issues or are they simply a marketing exercise in the creation of 'feel good'? We have seen previously that tinkering with procurement is not sufficient by itself. If core 'incompetencies' are not tackled, then everything else is an irrelevance. Several of the current initiatives are considered below.

Prime contracting

The MoD's Construction Supply Network Project (CSNP) is a direct pilot procurement technique derived from the Egan ideals. Utilising the concepts of open communication and design group clusters, it is endeavouring to deliver the targets set out by Egan. It involves a wide range of academic and practice-based organisations to advise, monitor and record the effectiveness of the two pilot projects. However, a recent report by the Tavistock Institute (Interim Report Summary, *Building*, 19 March 1999) suggests that the prime Contractors are struggling with the cultural issues involved.

The CSNP design processes involve two highly commendable ideals:

1   early access by the design team to the Client/User;
2   a project brief developed from the Client's strategic goals into a form pro-
    moting understanding and a reflection of User requirements.

The Ministry of Defence prime contracting pilot projects are located at the Wattisham and Aldershot sites. A recent article on the subject of Design and Build
(*Building Design*, 29 October 1999, p. 10) noted the projects as successfully delivering some of the anticipated benefits, namely, the blockwork achieving a 30–100
per cent rise in productivity, with a three-fold increase in profits. Killfoyle also fore-
cast a cut in construction time of between 18 and 25 per cent.

Interviews with those involved in the process indicate that it has generally
been welcomed as a way of encouraging improvement from the perspective of
both Consultant and Employer. The amount of Consultant and Designer input
during the construction phase is recorded as being significantly lower than would
normally be expected, and is attributed to a better development of both brief and
design before the commencement of construction works.

The management technique involved in both pilot projects involves the use
of 'cluster teams', each responsible for particular elements or subsections of the
work. Each in turn is led by an appropriate profession or contractor. The concept
of appropriate leaders for appropriate teams has much to be commended, but it
is clear that this is new territory for many. Consequently the effectiveness of
cluster leadership is variable, as organisations used to 'being led' are coming to
terms with the inevitable conflicts and difficulties that leadership brings with it.

Briefing by the MoD has been much more intensive, and certainly has commenced with an increased level of strategic input. Ultimately, however, it relies
upon prescriptive space standards with little or no zero-based objective analysis.
The early involvement of Users has been encouraged and the formal project
sponsor, or Employer's team leader, appointed to reconcile inevitable conflicting
requirements. At the point of interpretation, however, it is the traditional Architect that has the key responsibility for translation of brief into design. In reality,
input by cluster leaders tends to be cost or value focused.

One organisation heavily involved with prime contracting believes that the
primary driver encouraging such methodology is 'Client satisfaction and continuity
of work'. It is unfortunate, then, that the MoD are perpetuating the competitive
first stage of the procurement process together with the highly formalised short-
listing procedure. Lessons learnt from the pilot projects across the whole raft of
professionals and contractors will not be automatically reusable in the future. The
Defences Estates version of supply chain management is struggling, therefore, as
despite acknowledged benefits Contractors note (*Building*, 21 January 2000) that
there is insufficient continuity to ensure that teams remain together.

The key benefit of CSNP is intended to be seen in the form of motivation,
in the context of shared reward. The pilot projects are adopting alternative strategies in this context but clearly there is a long way to go before there is shared
reward in terms of real financial benefit for all. The issues of agendas and secret
knowledge, despite the 'open' approach, are still clear, with bid prices being
restricted from some team members.

The Defence Estates' head of quality, Clive Kane, was quoted (*Architects Journal*, 3 February 2000, p. 38) as saying 'we will never hire a Consultant ever again'. Relating to direct appointments this may be true; the implication that key professions can be 'dismissed' is not intended, but the statement can easily be misinterpreted in this way. Indeed the role of the Designer within the supply chain is currently receiving significant attention.

Following good Egan ideals, the second annual conference of the Design and Build Foundation focused on 'better by design'. One consideration posed the question: 'how designers can be better integrated into the project?' The pilot projects at Wattisham and Aldershot were described by Killfoyle in the context of supply chain management. His report emphasised the potential advantage of a single point responsibility but, much to the concern of some Contractors, it noted that there was no reason why Consultants should not take the lead as the Prime Contractors (Cook, *Building*, 29 October 1999, p. 18). Proposed payment provisions, however, would appear to make untenable the concept of the Consultant as 'prime contractor', except for a very few, due to the cash flow implications in relation to the structure of most Consultants (Cook, *Building*, 29 October 1999, p. 18). Innovation is making leaps forward but procedure and 'committee' thinking would appear to be acting as a restraint – probably a genuine case of two steps forward and one step back.

Despite elements of genuine innovation, the toolbox of supply chain management techniques that have been developed, nevertheless, retains an intensity of effort in the physical delivery of the project. Most importantly the process still retains the traditional interpretation of the Client brief and the space budget by traditional singular professions. CSNP does create the potential for harmony, shared goals, values and motive for all involved in the project, but fails to identify adequately one potentially key participant – the facility manager.

Lord McAlpine (McAlpine, *Building*, 16 July 1999) notes that prime contracting is really no different to turnkey D and B, such as employed on power stations, involving a consortium of Clients and a range of Contractors and Consultants. He appropriately concludes that prime contracting is an excellent concept, but only for projects that lend themselves to that approach, and not all do.

Performance indicators

1999 has seen the Egan ideals promoted again by the Construction Industry Board and the DETR under the 'Construction Best Practice Programme'. The programme has involved the production of guides, dealing with many of the concepts discussed in this book, including IT, culture, teamwork, briefing, partnering and 'lean' techniques. The heart of the programme is founded upon the idea of key performance indicators.

In keeping with good benchmark management, the underlying concept is measurement. Indeed, the documentation uses the catch-phrase 'Measurement is only the start – now you need to act'. This identifies the nub of the problem. Hard-edged issues such as time and cost can be relatively easily plotted onto charts, and data is easily obtainable. Less easy to measure are issues of Employer satisfaction. The 'Construction Best Practice Programme' includes provision for the measurement of such satisfaction, but fails to define any satisfactory criteria for the measurement. It refers to the 'finished product', but so often this means the quality of the wallpaper! It is good, however, to see an indicator for the element of service related both to Contractors and Consultants. Again, it is emphasised that the 'How?' is equally important as the 'What?' and can be highly instrumental in closing the performance gap.

The 'Construction Best Practice Programme' is predominantly aimed at the overall total construction cycle; it sees the project as the finished facility. Surveys clearly show, however, that much of the industry's problem, and the performance gap itself, is frequently derived at a much earlier stage when fundamental strategic briefing and design decisions are being made. The Egan argument for bringing contractors earlier into the cycle may offer benefits in terms of cost control and build-ability, but does little to deal with the fundamental root cause of inefficient, inappropriate or obsolete facilities. If the proposed facility is responding only to part of an organisation's need, or only to the immediate need, then the benefit of process improvements may only be transitory.

The Construction Industry Council (*Building*, 27 February 2000) at the time of writing is proposing to produce key performance indicators (KPIs) for design. Although service is included, the KPIs for construction and sustainability have tended to be concentrated on the hard issues. KPIs for design will, however, in the words of Chairman Dixon need to reconcile 'the intangible and tangible'. The harder aspects, such as customer satisfaction, accessibility and environmental issues have comparatively easy metrics compared with the more subjective judgements that may be relevant to building ambience and style. As the 60 working members of the group endeavour to establish a range of indicators, the Construction Industry Council Chairman, Robin Nicholson, honestly observes that he 'would not underestimate the difficulty of judging such things, but it is needed'. Undoubtedly, much debate will be required before any universally accepted formula is agreed.

Model project pact

Part of the Construction Industry Board's documentation on best practice and 1999 key performance indicators is the development of the 'model project pact'. This contains a variety of commendable ideals that describe fair practice and sound teamwork. The fact that there is a need for such a document to be distributed sadly reflects the lack of co-operation and trust that would appear to be commonplace.

It is important to put these issues into perspective. Clearly much dissatisfaction with projects exists, but it is suggested that by far the majority of project teams, now and for many years past, have committed to a project with the intention of delivering all of the nine issues identified in this current pact. The primary intention, 'to meet the needs and expectations for this project', is surely the intention of all reputable members of any Employer, Consultant or Contractor organisation, other than the most committed 'cowboy'.

In common with many improvement systems, the pact fails to deliver the provision of 'how', in reference to briefing the team, and to project briefing in terms of strategic concept and detailed design. Milestones and check lists are insufficient to ensure a seamless transfer of concepts and expectations.

The pact refers to the building of a balanced workforce and the seeking of continuous improvement with the appropriate research. Again, both are commendable but cannot work in isolation within the confines of a single everyday project. The maintenance of a balanced workforce, within the Employer, Consultant or the Contractor organisation, demands a continuous flow of projects. Partnering is intended to provide this facility by building ongoing relationships. It is unfortunately only available to those Employers that have ongoing construction projects. 'One-off' projects form a significant part of the industry and by their nature preclude partnering with an Employer beyond the single project. It is this interruption that also disturbs the pact's aim of 'continuous improvement'. Far too frequently both Consultants and Employers repeat mistakes of the past, due predominantly to the inability of 'one-off project teams' to pass on lessons learnt. Techniques must be developed for the retention of knowledge, and the conversion of tacit to explicit knowledge is critical for progress. This issue is expanded in Chapter 8.

Private Finance Initiative

Not unlike partnering and prime contracting, the 1990s has seen the renaissance of the Private Finance Initiative (PFI). PFI is essentially based on the subscriptions concept used by the Victorians and probably earlier, regardless of the current title of which there are several! This established concept of private investment in public facilities has been formalised into a model relevant to the construction industry. Although not strictly innovation in the sense of having 'improved quality' as its prime objective, it does have, as a by-product and by necessity, the need to involve contractors and sub-contractors from the outset. It does consider whole-life costing and it involves an array of innovative relationships between Employer, Consultants and Contractors. It is nevertheless primarily the subject of financial drivers.

For real quality improvements to be realised, the initial stages of the PFI process require major overhaul. Speculative input by certain members of the PFI team, particularly Contractors and Consultants, cannot be a sound basis upon which to commence long-term projects. Concerns regarding design development and the strategic input have been discussed at length elsewhere; similarly, issues of motivation and the Egan concept of improved profit levels appear to be equally contrary to PFI in practice. Systems must be developed to ensure that all contributors are reimbursed in a way that relates to the risk. Employers cannot expect the level of design development and strategic thinking that is necessary for true innovation, if Contributors are expected to work at risk and then possibly in the future have the opportunity of payment at a level commensurate with 'no risk' commissions. In reply to these comments the government are currently calling for a higher level of design quality in these projects.

The political and economic profile of the twenty-first century would appear to offer an expanding opportunity for PFI as buildings are increasingly seen as commodities. It retains at present, however, all of the potential performance gaps, and a few more, that are seen in more traditional forms of procurement.

Benchmarking

Despite the somewhat passé image of benchmarking, there remains a commitment to the concept. As often reported, the delay between innovation, best/good practice and common usage can be 20 years; benchmarking is no exception. The 'Construction Industry Best Practice' key performance indicators are essentially a benchmarking system. The variety of successful benchmarking organisations and publications bears witness to an increasing awareness amongst all organisations of these concepts. Whereas 'best practice' organisations benchmarked their own processes some 20 years ago, the concept is now reaching a more popularist level.

When considering expectation and realisation, benchmarking clearly has a place. It can serve to raise a profile of service and product quality in relation to the industry in general. But it frequently fails to deliver the promised benefits, due to the inability to set uniform standards between those delivering and those receiving.

Practice shows that benchmarking frequently concentrates on the hard issues of service, quite simply because the metrics for the softer issues, the 'how' issues, are much more difficult to define. Again, we return to the problem of the Employer, inexperienced and without frequent demands upon the construction industry. Such Employers may not have embarked in the past upon a given type of project, and therefore cannot benchmark their own performance. Each new step is a new world. It is therefore essential that appropriate guidance is available to enable each new step to be made in the right direction. While much of the Latham/Egan concept may be commendable, and to that extent appropriate to the inexperienced Employer, it is also equally certain that it is much more difficult to implement in a one-off situation. It is therefore necessary to consider strategies that are more widely applicable.

The benchmarking of quality, as opposed to finite acts, has always proven difficult; design is no exception. As part of attempts to relocate Architects in the integrated supply chain, the Tavistock Institute has in draft documentation (1999) offered definitions and measurements of design quality. Design quality is seen as 'the ability to delight' and 'design' is seen as the value added to a project. The proposed defining elements of 'design quality' were described in Chapter 2, but much in the same way that the Construction Industry Council are debating their design KPIs, the Tavistock Institute foresee the agreement of metrics as difficult.

Design and Build

As discussed in Chapter 5, certain anomalies developed within the responses from Design and Build Contractors. These 'anomalies' revolved around issues of role and the management of the interfaces between the various contracting parties. Historically, the concept of Design and Build provided Employers with a 'one stop' solution capable of providing a fixed project for a fixed price in a fixed timescale. The experience of many Employers, however, shows disillusionment with this procurement route. Much of this disillusionment is centred around the failure to realise expectation primarily in terms of function and aesthetic.

Partnering encouraged by the Egan and Latham concept has provided significant incentive for Design and Build Contractors to improve their methodology and, as a consequence, their service to Employers. It is clear, however, that there are wide ranging levels of quality and, therefore, experience on behalf of all parties. Design and Build contracting falls into two categories:

1   contractors genuinely specialising in this method of procurement;
2   traditional contractors purporting to specialise in this procurement method.

The second group frequently use management techniques and personnel that are directly derived from their traditional contracts and attempt to emulate those Contractors who do genuinely employ specialist construction teams and process managers. Of those that do genuinely have appropriate management, few actually directly employ design staff. As a consequence they resort to the use of private practice. It is at this point where the real anomalies begin to be exposed. In this scenario the Contractor becomes an Employer.

Within the most focused Design and Build Contractors, in terms of management, two Employer interfaces develop. First, that of the paymaster/user Employer with Design and Build design co-ordinator and then, separately, an interface between the design co-ordinator and his externally appointed professional team. The potential for failures in communication as the game of Chinese whispers develops is inevitable. It is quite common, however, to see Design and Build Contractors take a step back when the commission is secured, and allow the external Consultants to liaise directly with the paymaster/user Employer, as demonstrated in Figure 5.7. This inevitably leads to conflicts and a complete blurring of the Employer/employee interface. It is the failure of the Design and Build contractors generally to appreciate their role as Employers as opposed to Contractors that can contribute to the potential of a performance gap in this procurement scenario.

Prescriptive registration procedures are currently being adopted by the Design and Build Foundation. Registration will be dependant upon conformity to certain criteria and payment of a fee. The proposal is being extended to Consultants wishing to be on the register. There must be a question as to whether this will provide a genuine measure of quality or something more akin to membership of one of the many trade bodies to which both Consultants and Contractors subscribe (*Building*, 29 October 1999).

Despite the great enthusiasm for the process of Design and Build, some contractors honestly admit that they are struggling with the need to eradicate 'fundamental problems'. The same Contractor cited one problem as being 'the need to determine prices before design is fully developed'. This returns very much to the comments made in previous Chapters, describing lack of design development and overly short inception periods that tend to accompany most projects (White, *Building*, 22 October 1999, p. 18).

Design and Build can be an appropriate and effective form of procurement. It does have the ability to provide at least some of the benefits extolled by Egan, but it is not a panacea for all ills. The fundamental issues of communication between Employer and Consultant must be addressed. The issues of translation and agenda must be opened up much more widely than is evident at present.

Partnering

Partnering has been referred to (Cox and Townsend 1998, p. 32) as 'the latest fad' to emerge as the way forward. It has been suggested that it was a subjective presumption in Latham and referred to as 'bare foot empiricism'. Cox and Townsend suggested that it has no theoretical framework to it, it is merely a reaction. It is fact that it borrows heavily from the Japanese way of working, the *keiretsu* structure. It is also fact that the Japanese system has been fraying at the edges due to recent commercial pressure within the country.

There appears to be a consensus of opinion that a multitude of agendas will occur within any team. The definition of the 'multi-headed' Client supports the existence of multiple agendas within the Employer. There is clearly no reason why this duplicity cannot continue through all contributors. Richardson (1996, p. 60) suggests that 'all prospective Clients have a hidden agenda', and there may be a series of issues they want to have addressed but are unable to articulate in a way that can be translated into a building.

Two parallel surveys covering current practice and Client are reviewed by Touche Ross (RIBA 1993), and a number of key themes identified, noting that Architects and Clients approached a project with different aspirations and priorities. These divergent sets of interests ensure the uneasy relationship between parties described in Chapter 4. Patey (Delargy, *Building*, 10 September 1999, p. 50) believes that if only 90 per cent of the workforce supports partnering then the other 10 per cent will bring the whole structure down, so it reverts to old methods of horse-trading with suppliers.

Both Client and Architects involved with the first MoD CSNP projects agree that long-term supply chains reinforce and fully utilise the Architects' skills. It is noteworthy, however, that the current shortlist for the first 'follow-on' major MoD project does not, at the present time, include the same Contractor and team on the shortlist. Clearly, long-term relationships beyond a single project have some way to develop within a formal public procurement programme.

Teamwork in the Wal-Mart sense places high demands upon Consultants and subsequent Design and Build teams and involves 'fines' for deviation from the prescriptive Wal-Mart specification. It is alleged (Pearson, *Building*, 19 November 1999, p. 59) that Consultants are rewarded by low fees, the threat of fines, but with a strong expectation that there will be a focused team dynamic. The concept of standardisation and improvements in performance certainly are in line with the UK's Egan ideals, but it is difficult to reconcile the concepts of low fees and blame culture with team dynamic.

The Rover group have adopted what they call 'adaptive partnering' in respect of construction projects; it includes three levels:

1   single source contracting;
2   preferred suppliers;
3   arms-length arrangements.

The chief driver is cost, closely followed by a need for consistency in quality. Written partnership agreements include reference to open-book contracting and agreed profit levels. Overruns have allegedly reduced from 50 per cent to 5 per cent over a 5-year period.

Clearly, life in the construction industry is changing. The survey carried out by Davis Langdon Consultancy on behalf of Robert Fleming Securities (Chevin, *Building*, 26 November 1999, p. 20), and based on experienced Employers, demonstrated real change at the end of the twentieth century. Competitive tendered work accounted for 61 per cent of the respondents' workload, as opposed to 87 per cent in 1995. Similarly, the percentage of negotiated or partnered work has risen by 3 per cent over the past 5 years. There is clearly a move towards the repetitive use of Contractors, and Clients noted that they felt that this has reduced litigation. Unfortunately the survey does not indicate the form of contract procurement and there is no reference to the design process or indeed professionals, other than the contractor as such. It is nevertheless a clear indication that, certainly amongst the most informed Employers, traditional competitive tendering is declining. There would appear to be a steady flow of private sector Clients signing up to Partnership or framework agreements (*Architects Journal*, 3 February 2000, p. 38).

Standardisation

The Chartered Institute of Purchasing and Supply have quoted (Cox and Townsend 1998, p. 258) that UK projects involve 20–30 per cent more manhours than equivalent projects in the USA. Three solutions to this problem include:

1   standardisation – involving repetition of components and finished product;
2   pre-assembly – either on-site or off-site;
3   modularisation – either sub-components or total volumetric construction.

In addition, any of the above concepts of standardisation in respect to specification, product or material can be applied at a variety of levels:

1   generic – universal interchangeable products;
2   national – accepted norms within a defined geographical area;
3   Employer specific – typically found in retail or other multiple site organisa-
    tions, or those having specific industry standards, e.g. MoD;
4   manufacturer – accepted industry or available specification/product;
5   project – specific standards adopted for a single or group of projects.

There is clearly a range of 'standardisation' concepts and a range of projects to
which they are applicable. The 'bespoke' design will still have a number of genuine
standard components straight from the production line, for example mechanical
and electrical fittings. At the other extreme, there is the fully completed building
often associated with temporary offices and classrooms. In between is the potential area for increased use of pre-assembly, modularisation and standard products.
The breadth of standardisation runs in parallel to the fabrication concept. 'Agile'
systems are associated with customised products and flexible systems to gain efficiency, but maintain the ability to reconfigure. 'Lean' techniques are generally
more rigid and gain efficiency from repetitive process. The potential from both
systems can aid gaps in reliability and expectation in terms of function and cost.

There remains, however, a cultural bias in favour of the 'one-off'. The legacy
from failed system building of the 1960s remains a strong influence in the minds of
both Employer and Consultant. US retailer Wal-Mart sees no value in the 'one-
off'; concepts of standardisation and continuous cost reduction are certainly deep
rooted (Pearson, *Building*, 19 November 1999, p. 59). According to Bob Simpson,
the head of Asda development, Wal-Mart's latest acquisition, the US technique
demands a highly prescriptive specification and a large element of standardisation,
that includes everything down to steel sections.

Amec Construction unveiled a new standard 'fast track classroom' aimed at
the School PFI market at the Labour conference in October 1999. It does
respond to demands of standardisation, and hence of cost advantages and speed.
Descriptions of the classroom have compared the structural concept to that of
Holiday Inns and prisons. The latter are not popularly recognised for their aesthetic delight. Similarly, it would appear difficult to find delight in the published
visual of the classroom. Standardisation, speed of erection and value for money
surely does not have to mean that aesthetic design is ignored. This is an excellent
example to counteract the view put forward by some (Harding, *Building*, 1
October 1999, p. 31), suggesting that there is no great role for Architects within
the process.

Nevertheless, standard buildings take a step closer as construction managers
Mace (White, *Building*, 19 November 1999, p. 18) develop a set of 'off-the-shelf'
buildings. These are predesigned but have the potential for customisation. Their
use of 3D models and full-scale mock ups and samples is considered to be a way
of avoiding a performance gap in terms of expectation and realisation, as well as
having practical benefits in terms of lead-in times and cost.

McDonalds, the fast food provider, found that traditional Consultants
appointments can result in up to 40 per cent over-provision of space (Cox and
Townsend 1998, p. 141). Much of this is due to lack of marketing input, and poor

communication with end users. The new approach began as a technical fix but percolated into management. The approach involved standardisation and modularisation. McDonalds now find that 50 per cent of cost for the new development is based around the assembler and the final 50 per cent of the cost is with the component supplier. Fit-for-purpose supply relationships are the standard, and suppliers and assemblers sit side by side with an in-house concept design team. McDonalds (Cox and Townsend 1998, p. 143) advise that the 27-week contract period in 1986 is now reduced to an average 36 days, with a corresponding 50 per cent reduction in maintenance costs plus consistent quality of product.

The announcement by the Post Office (*Contract Journal*, 26 January 2000, p. 3), that it sees no value in appointing a design team for future projects, as they would mostly be built to a standard design, would appear to miss much of the value that design can bring to any project. The product may be repetitive in the year 2000, but standard solutions have great potential for becoming the straight jackets to future change. If standard solutions are to have real future value then the design input needs to be raised rather than reduced. The antithesis of the PFI classroom referred to above is the 'Akademy' classroom developed by Portakabin and the architects Cottrell and Vermeulen, demonstrating that standard prefabricated solutions can and *must* include a high level of 'design'.

Long-term adaptability must be an integral component of any 'standardised' solution. The high level of embedded energy in most buildings, and the associated investment, demands a long life, despite the need for a regular strip to the skeleton for adaptation and change. The concept of 'one building' (Bartlett 1999, p. 40) to fit all and provide multi-use class and multi-spacial options should be the ideal to be pursued. The building must be designed to come apart so as to be adaptable for the changes referred to above and even, for example in the retail industry, to be adaptable for the whims of 'fashion'.

The concept of standardisation and the need to avoid reinventing the wheel have taxed all individual organisations, whether Consultant, Contractor or Employer, for many years. Examples of individual companies standardising information and providing it in an accessible format, are commonplace. Numerous organisations use intranets or internet websites to provide IT-based information throughout their *own* organisation. However it is the wider distribution of information, as opposed to 'local hoarding', that is the challenge for the future.

This need has not gone unnoticed and attempts being made to address it. As a start, the Building Research Establishment (BRE) is currently exploring the concept of a national standards details library, offering registered users a searchable base of details and drawings in a variety of CAD formats. The concept is sound but is practically fraught with difficulties. Technical protocol, reliability, and liability are but a few of the issues involved. Effort and subsequent cost and time is required from all parties to ensure the success of such knowledge distribution.

Appropriate standardisation and computerisation is acknowledged as having a positive benefit, by allowing the production of an integrated design, using input from a variety of suppliers. But it is also suggested (Bartlett 1999, p. 45) that IT can be the end of standardisation. Computer aided manufacturing techniques have the potential to allow much greater expression of design via the simple techniques that are available for translating design directly into the manufactured product. Standardisation should perhaps be understood as 'prefabrication'. The easy production of complex forms that cannot be made by constructors with 'hammer and a saw' (Bartlett 1999, p. 46) may allow significant innovation and design purity. The myriad of architectural 'cover up' components used in most projects, could become a thing of the past as designers are able to procure items that really fit.

It is clear that initiatives promoting 'standardisation' have much potential, but it is essential to realise that if long-term benefits are to be realised, then much higher levels of design are required. The breadth of 'standardisation' is enormous and certainly little to do with accepting repetitive compromise solutions. To maximise the advantages of standard products, modularisation and pre-assembly in respect of both components and assemblies, the design process requires innovation and appropriate resourcing.

Information technology

Just as the construction industry is coming to terms with the production and distribution of data and drawings in CAD formats, the world is about to change again. Although CAD, word processing, and spreadsheet applications are commonplace they are by no means universal in construction projects. Where they are used, they retain very much a traditional format, in the sense of replicating hand-produced data. A typical CAD drawing produced at the beginning of the twenty-first century would certainly be readable in a hard format by nineteenth century counterparts.

Three-dimensional object-based systems will become everyday tools, and will provide a complete interaction between design, procurement and implementation. Ray Crottey (Delargy, *Building*, 2 July 1999, p. 48) is passionate that 3-D modelled projects will ensure that buying a building will become as predictable as buying a car. The benefits of conveying conceptual design to lay people by 3-D modelling is clear, but it is obviously a seductive medium that has its own limitations. Full virtual reality, at a cost, has the clear ability to stun the senses and appeal to the heart.

It is no more and no less than a tool. The resolution of the primary issues of communication, agenda, culture etc. is the starting point if the potential of IT systems is to be released. Crottey also considers that 'old skills will die and new ones emerge, general contracting will go and you will end up with Project Managers and franchise installers/suppliers'. At this point there is a close relationship between IT and 'lean'/'agile' techniques, utilising a range of 'standardisation' initiatives.

The concept of reducing the burden of paper and duplication of effort that is evident throughout the procurement programme can only be commended. It demands, however, the cascading of knowledge and technology throughout the industry. It requires a level of common protocol and understanding. Even at current simplistic levels of use, traditional computerised systems appear to provide far too many application difficulties for 'mechanical' man.

Resourcing

The late 1980s, and most of the 1990s, saw a procurement system led by competitive tendering. EEC and UK Government procedures and regulations have reinforced this message. The compulsory tendering procedure of the public sector, often culminating in the Official Journal of European Communities (OJEC) list, is the common model. Tendering then often cascades through the invited Contractors, who in turn seek tenders from Consultants and Subcontractors. In this scenario, it is not uncommon for dozens of Consultants and Subcontractors to be busily preparing tenders for a single project. Apart from the inevitable demotivation this experience causes, it is also extremely wasteful of resources. Commonly the profit available for a single project is far less than the cumulative costs of all those tendering.

A survey regarding fees (Garvin 1988, p. 43) by the Association of Consulting Engineers concluded that competitive fees had given rise to:

1   significantly less consideration of design alternatives;
2   less checking;
3   general quality reduction.

Employers interviewed as part of the 1998 survey agreed totally with the third point, often acknowledging that their own procurement systems were much to blame. Open discussion of these issues between Employer and Consultant is rare, but is implied by several sources (Preiser 1993, p. 432) relating to timescales and quality.

Low wages and little standardisation means that the UK has the lowest input costs into construction but the highest output cost within Europe (Office of Science and Technology 1995, p. 9). This is considered to be a disincentive to innovation, and simply maintains the commercial agenda as high profile. Procurement under European law has for some years hindered public sector procedures. The lack of flexibility is extremely problematic and has caused great difficulty in dealing with post-tender discussions to avoid 'negotiation' which is contrary to EU rules (Minogue, *Building*, 19 November 1999). New EU reforms, due in 2000, should allow much closer parallel with the Egan agenda of partnering methods, and avoid the current 'illegal negotiation'.

Egan proposes less dependence upon competitive price tendering, increased profit levels and increased standardisation. It is clear that a lot of effort in the construction industry is being made. Egan, together with many other contributors, has been instrumental in raising the profile, and initiating this debate. The primary motivator accepted by the task force is profit. Clearly, adequate profit levels and performance gaps are related. What price is an Employer willing to put upon Design development/quality? The discussion returns to the issue of defining appropriate quality at the outset, and the 'Rolls for a Mini' syndrome. Disregarding money, however, there are strategies available to maximise the effectiveness of finite resources. Current systems fail to optimise commercially constrained resources, but these can be changed. Chapter 8 will consider improvement strategies in this area.

Conclusion – alternatives or hot air?

What are Egan and the current initiatives achieving? Unquestionably, profile, research and improvement, in a general sense. What is of concern, however, is that despite all this attention, the fundamental relationships, forms of communication and information databases remain essentially unchanged.

As part of the spreading of the Egan principle the Department of Environment, Transport and Regions has issued a directive that all social housing, developed by Housing Associations, must be '100 per cent Egan compliant' by the year 2004 (Martin, *Building Design*, 5 November 1999, p. 3). It is curious to see that such Draconian edicts are necessary to ensure what is ultimately just good practice. Bernard Hunt, Director of the National House Building Council, optimistically envisages that management processes will achieve the prescriptive improvements noted by Egan. Encouragingly, he observes that good practice is required insofar as more post-occupancy evaluation will be necessary to ensure that the ultimate users, namely the tenants, gain increased satisfaction.

Employer, Consultant, Contractor and all contributors to the design process must develop a wider, more flexible selection of tools to facilitate the process. The crux is the translation of expectation into reality. It is quite acceptable to take lessons gleaned from reports and initiatives relating to current best practice, but to make meaningful progress, the fundamental issues must be addressed.

It is easy for distorted views to be presented as fact. For example, argument in a recent article (Harding, *Building*, 1 October 1999) on the issue of design faults in relation to the Egan concepts, raises many fair comments. But it includes a 'side swipe' at one section of the design team, namely the Architects, stating that 'only a small proportion of Architects have even heard of Sir John Egan's report'. Unquestionably that is incorrect, and merely speculation. Produced at the same time, a research project (Somogyi 1999) indicated that 72 per cent of Architects were fully aware of it, with some 59 per cent attempting to adhere to its proposals. The many commendable comments in this article are overshadowed by 'blame culture'. It is characteristic of the industry as a whole. If the industry is to move forward, it is essential that each contributor to a project is respected for their skills and expertise. It must be recognised that no one contributor has any natural right to lead the team, or indeed has any all-encompassing skill that may exclude another team member.

Traditionally the Architect has been subjected to criticism, as the expectation and role of the profession has changed. Approaches that simply 'draw up Clients' ideas' at one extreme, or seek to gain the applause of the architectural press at the other extreme, have been equally derided. In part, due to commercial restraints that have been placed upon practice, design development, quality and management have frequently failed expectation. Whether, in relation to restricted fee levels, these services provide value for money, is another issue.

It has been suggested (Phippen, *Building*, 23 July 1999, p. 39) that the Architect's role is marginalised and the traditional 'pure' Architect can only survive in the context of a broadly based professional institute, covering possibly the RIBA and the RICS. Conversely, the report by the Tavistock Institute, referred to previously, and presented as a draft to the Government in December 1999, proposes that the Architect has a much more valuable contribution in terms of adding value to a project and providing real design quality. The Government's interest in assessing the role of Architects in the construction supply chain is encouraging for the profession and can only assist in the resolution of the 'bickering' that has plagued the industry for so long.

As the MoD continues to explore options in its prime contracting initiative, alternatives to the traditional systems of 'retentions', as incentive to performance, are questioned. Proposed 'fitness for purpose' clauses have been met by significant objection, based primarily upon reaction from the insurance industry. It does not appear to be unreasonable for obligations within the construction industry to embrace fitness for purpose much in the same way as the concept of merchantable quality is a mainstay of the retail industry. Demands are also heard in the industry for changes in the way buildings are insured in respect of defects. The idea may appear sound, but little progress can be made until clear definitions of 'fitness' and 'purpose' are achievable. 'The transparency' referred to elsewhere in this book is essential. There are no members of the project team who are genuinely clairvoyant.

Very little of what has been described as alternative strategies can be condemned. It may well be that there are arguments regarding quantum, popular relevance, and certainly questions as to whether these 'new' alternatives are indeed new. But there remain a number of fundamental unanswered questions:

- What is the appropriate motivation?
- How do you retain knowledge gained through project development?
- How does one integrate the multi-headed Employer, bringing together user, paymaster and manager?
- How do you ensure that translation of expectation into reality is successful?

The list could continue. It is necessary to develop an understanding of those issues that have been demonstrated to go consistently wrong. Based on the 1998 survey and the interpretation in Chapter 5, it is possible to develop strategies that pre-empt the problem. Measurement of performance is certainly of benefit to the next project. However, the establishment of a culture to *avoid* disappointment is a much more preferable strategy. The next chapter concentrates on the key issues that have been discussed and sets out strategies to enable significant improvement.

8 Strategies for the future

Introduction

We have seen the existence of a gap between expectation and realisation in building projects demonstrated by survey, interview and reference to previous studies. The focus of the study, the communication interface between Employer and Consultant, has identified a number of potential causes contributing to 'the project performance gap'. It can be seen from survey respondents' comments and interview transcripts that the gap between expectation and realisation is equally evident at the communication interfaces between Consultant and Contractor, Contractor and Employer and so on, some of which are shown in Figure 8.1. This is endorsed by a range of recent surveys and reports considering the construction industry as a whole.

This 1998 study has identified a number of key issues that contribute to the gap at the Consultant/Employer interface. These themes are summarised in the conclusion of Chapters 5 and 6. The scale and areas of the expectation/realisation gap are evident and factual. The key question facing both Employer, Consultant and indeed the entire construction industry is how these issues will be reconciled, and what steps can be adopted to improve the current situation. The initiatives and current responses described in Chapter 7 do unquestionably set in place a variety of tools, but the development of universal and sustained improvement demands a cultural shift for all involved.

The work of Whorf and Sapir (Davenport 1994) has shown how language and culture is a barrier to understanding. Levels of knowledge further compound the problem. Two-way translation by all involved in the design process and a common language is the key to a genuine understanding of expectation.

Many issues could be dismissed as 'communication' and, indeed, this is the critical element. However, these are clearly problems that have not been resolved over many years of current traditional practice. As previously noted, User Employers are increasingly concentrating on their own core business. As a result the need for communication channels between lay persons and external professionals is likely to increase, potentially exacerbating the current 'gaps'. For the purposes of considering these issues in terms of implications for current practice and futures, it is proposed that the issues raised in Chapter 5 are considered under three headings, as shown in Figure 8.2.

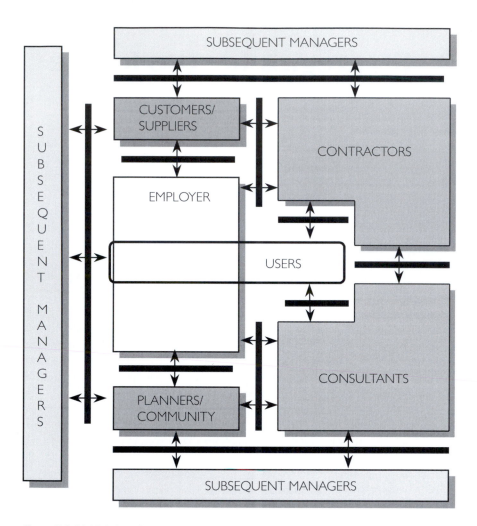

Figure 8.1 Multiple interfaces created by a project

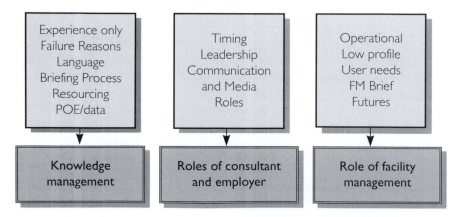

Figure 8.2 Discussion areas from themes of Chapter 5

Knowledge management

Basis of knowledge

Essentially the design and construction industry has a great deal of information and potential knowledge, but very little management. Similarly, most Employers have extensive levels of information as evidenced by the relevant specialist press (e.g. The Grocer, Retail Week, Shopping Centre, etc. to name but a few in the retail sector). Consultancy is similarly awash with excellent publications from the BRE, Building Services Research and Information Association (BSRIA), Chartered Institution of Building Services Engineers (CIBSE), as well as literally hundreds of regularly published journals. Bridging the gap between Employer and Consultant are published focus books and guidance notes issued by Government Quangos and specialists. Despite this extensive information background, both Consultants and Employers readily admit that experience is the primary basis for briefing and building design, and it is acknowledged that reference to 'the written word' is the 'last port of call'.

It is often the case that Employers may be venturing into the unknown, while their advisers and suppliers within the construction industry have 'seen it all before'. In such circumstances experience can clearly be of assistance but, equally, can be a major obstacle. It can be a barrier to innovation, and to the task of determining the Employer's true values and requirements, as opposed to smothering him with preconceived solutions.

The encoded nature of much data and poorly managed accessibility are primary reasons for the low usage. More than a technical 'fix' is needed, however, and a culture change is essential. Knowledge, as distinct from information, can be seen as either 'explicit' or 'tacit'. The former is that typically stored as a written procedure, and repetitively used by numerous organisations. 'Tacit' refers to knowledge that is practice-related and commonly known to individuals, but not recorded.

The use of tacit knowledge demands trust in the 'knowledge holder', but has potentially greater relevance to areas of uncertainty and innovation. One of the goals for Employers and Consultants alike is the transformation of areas of tacit knowledge into explicit, to allow the development of a shared base. For example, the tacit knowledge of the operative who knows that a particular configuration of workspace always needs adaptation after installation, must be transformed to a widely available feedback-note (explicit knowledge), advising that product 'X' requires modification before delivery. Figure 8.3 provides a matrix of uncertainty relating to the status of knowledge. Clearly increasing uncertainty demands innovation and increasingly tacit knowledge. In practice this requires testing and risk assessment in parallel with development. The management of risk, however, is much better founded upon a knowledge-based system as opposed to a global percentage contingency addition, which remains the common response.

The accepted minimal use of existing sources of explicit knowledge is attributable to three primary causes.

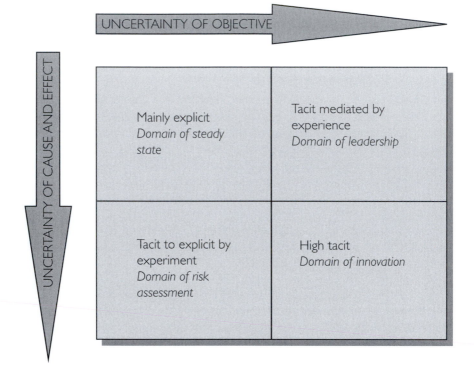

Figure 8.3 Matrix of uncertainty

1 Information is frequently 'encoded', making it readily accessible only to the particular focus group, whether it be an Employer sector or a Consultant sector, by virtue of its circulation, language and format.
2 Ready and convenient access to significant levels of information is denied to the vast majority of Employers and Consultants.
3 Frequently the given resource in terms of time and manpower at the outset of a project is insufficient or inappropriately programmed, and experience is the most readily available data base.

The review of literature and guidance notes demonstrates that there is a wide divergence in the language and format of such documentation. It appears to polarise between the simplistic and the technically complex. While academic text and papers may be impartial and objective, but technically complex, often practice-led guidance notes and documents are of particular focus *and* incorporate the sponsor's agenda.
    Knowledge management requires five steps:

1 identification – the determination of what is relevant, what is useful and what is mere clutter;
2 retention – methods for holding information in a situation that may have other pressures, change in personnel and more immediate goals;

3   conversion – consolidation of a disparate set of information sources that may include files, drawings and the minds of numerous contributors and stake-holders, tacit to explicit;
4   distribution – the dissemination of relevant information to all contributors and ultimately to the wider community, both within the construction industry and other Employers;
5   utilisation – ensuring that the distributed information is actually used: over-coming the 'personal experience' option as the first and only port of call, and avoidance of the 'not invented here' syndrome.

Information technology has clearly influenced the accessibility of information, and it is common for a great deal to be stored on CD ROMs within Consultancies. This again suffers the problems of having a selected content and frequently a commercial agenda attached to a limited distribution. Various authoritative quangos also produce information in this format, but it remains poorly referenced and autonomous.

In addition to the sources referred to above, there are an enormous number of websites purporting to provide information. Although structure and accessibility are the key to success, it is not a regulated internet that is required. This would inevitably stifle innovation and probably involve levels of censorship, again accompanied by a commercial agenda. The Building Research Establishment website opened in January 2000 and is based on a research grant from the European Commission. Their embryonic web-based library of standard drawings has great potential, but demands major shifts in the culture of the individual if barriers to distribution and utilisation are to be overcome. As this book concludes the BRE are juggling with the traditional problem associated with any library of drawings: if generic they may become simplistic and unreal, while 'real' details have the potential of restricted application. Acceptance of new 'building blocks' of knowledge is required by Employers and Consultants alike. Providing easy accessibility to a wide variety of data is a starting point.

Knowledge hubs

Experimentation with project hubs has started. Several examples of use by organisations such as W. S. Atkins, the Charter Partnership, Crest Homes and British Telecom are noted. The purpose of the project hub is to provide an information base on which all members of the team can work and to provide a co-ordinated library of 'managed knowledge'. Obviously such a system is dependent upon the quality of the knowledge available and entered as the project proceeds. Issues of security are manageable and the benefit quantifiable.

The concept of knowledge management has been developed against a background of increased IT literacy. IT can be seen as giving the opportunity to integrate the design process. The use, for example, of suppliers' design drawings as 'modlets' can be used to build up co-ordinated comprehensive design. Six steps are suggested (Bartlett 1999, p. 45) as a framework for the management of knowledge within a project environment.

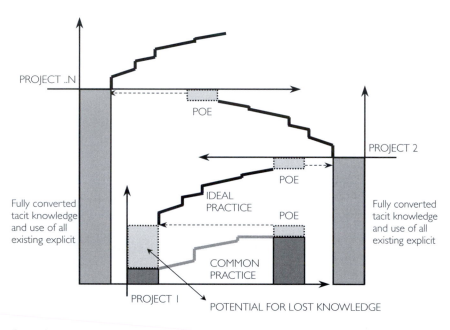

PROJECT ..N

POE

PROJECT 2

Fully converted
tacit knowledge
and use of all
existing explicit

IDEAL
PRACTICE

POE

POE

Fully converted
tacit knowledge
and use of all
existing explicit

COMMON
PRACTICE

PROJECT 1

POTENTIAL FOR LOST KNOWLEDGE

Figure 8.4 Learning between projects

1   Initiate a project website – this allows the central storage of both design and administrative data.
2   Provide server bases for all users, thus allowing 'thinner' software on user computers to minimise cost and conflict.
3   Implement an integrating language capable of overcoming traditional barriers between different IT systems, e.g. Java.
4   Introduce *managed* information servers, with systems to maximise dynamism, integration and development.
5   Provide 3D object-based architectural and engineering component modelling to produce fully functional models.
6   Provide life cycle integration – allowing the dissemination of information to building users, owners and the design team for both operational and learning purposes.

The technical issues and concepts referred to above are not a barrier, even to the most IT illiterate. It is the cultural shift that requires the real effort.

Building on the model of Figure 5.18, the model shown in Figure 8.4 demonstrates the idea of continuous knowledge growth (referred to in Japan as *kaizen*) through inter-project knowledge hubs. The next step is provision of a national or international hub of knowledge readily accessible and having consistent language and level of authority. *Information* bases, such as the BRE website, referred to previously are developing, but *knowledge* bases of any value remain in the private domain of the project. It is clear that there are unco-ordinated databases of building performance, postoccupancy evaluations (POE) and design analysis, but until this is more readily accessible little general use can be made of this knowledge base. Again commercial issues enter the arena and it is suggested that if this hub of public knowledge should be controlled by a commercial organisation, then levels of bias and exclusion may occur. Conversely, the other extreme is the example of the Internet which contains extensive information but is completely uncontrolled and without consistent authority. Richardson's (*Architects Journal*, 26 February 1998, p. 56) vision of a network economy, that is a culture change rather than a technical fix, is ultimately inevitable. But if it is to be universally available, then much development is required.

The need for the availability of good building evaluation is referred to by Sir John Egan. This study concurs, and it can be seen that repetition based upon 'experience plus 5 per cent' will be perpetuated until such a source of knowledge exists. Zero-based briefing has the potential for efficient, effective and innovative design but will only become reality with appropriate resources and managed knowledge. Zero-based briefing, however, does not imply the continuous prototype of zero-based design, which is naturally the antithesis of 'lean' systems.

Post-occupancy evaluation and much of the knowledge management discussed and referred to as 'project-based information' is of a predominantly hard nature. Much emphasis has been placed elsewhere upon the issue of 'how'. It does not seem unreasonable therefore that both Employers, Consultants and indeed all other suppliers should undertake post-occupancy evaluation in respect of the delivery of the service as a two-way exercise. The concept of 'Client care' is increasingly used by a number of service organisations as a method of maintaining loyalty. Certainly, the basic concept of partnership should facilitate the ongoing evaluation of such service. Guidance (Collard, *Building*, 10 September 1999, p. 75) suggests that face-to-face interviewing is the most effective method and, although obviously expensive, it should provide the best long-term reward. Similar recommendations include gaining such feedback from a variety of perspectives within both the Employer and Consultant organisation. The variety of expectations and agendas previously described indicates that feedback that excludes Users and subsequent managers will have little merit. Praise from the finance director may be appreciated and even well deserved, but it will not add to the body of knowledge in respect of, for example, ergonomic issues or the way the service was delivered.

Unquestionably *some* readers will be saying that thorough project review is their normal practice. I would report that these readers are almost exclusively Consultants and I would suggest that few Employers seek appraisal of *their* performance, in respect of outsourced project team membership. It may well be that for the one-off Client there is little short-term gain; nevertheless appraisals should be capable of enhancing improvement in whatever context. It has also been suggested that even within those good practice organisations carrying out service level research, few disseminate the information throughout the organisation. How often is it held at a middle or high level while a junior member of staff repeats the same service delivery on the next project?

Case studies (Chessun 1999) have demonstrated that a body of knowledge always exists at the end of a project. In none of these case studies, however, was knowledge passed on to future managers. As clearly seen, there is a gulf between operational and project management.

It has been observed (*Architects Journal*, 7 October 1999, p. 37) that the authors of PROBE (Post Occupancy Review of Buildings and their Engineering) could easily have focused on designer/technical features in relation to occupant satisfaction. They note however that it is much more complex and demands the bringing together of both design and management. Clearly any dissemination of POE data needs treating carefully, as concentration on the hardware supplied by Architects and Designers is equally dependent upon the software supplied by effective management. If the potential of *kaizen*, (in Figure 8.4), is to be realised, then the criticality of knowledge management and a 'learning' environment must be embraced.

Resourcing and standardisation

A study completed in 1989 concluded that 25 per cent of Employers were self-critical with frequent reference to 'less haste more speed'. The same report refers to these communication problems being due to, in the words of the 1962 Emmerson report, the 'divorce of design from production'. Little has changed as we begin the twenty-first century.

The question of time was raised by numerous respondents of the Authors 1998 study and again has been referred to in recent government reports. The 'lean' production techniques described by Egan have been treated with dismay by some designers, but in reality standardisation of many products and components would have no detrimental effect upon a designer's creativity. For example, it is anecdotally noted that Architects in the USA have a choice of six water closets, whereas the UK Architect has to select from over 40!

The subtleties of 'Agile' and 'Lean' concepts have been discussed in Chapter 7. Consultants or Employers cannot afford to ignore these ideas, if they genuinely seek improved design development. If adequate resourcing, in a commercial context, is to be achieved for design development, then project teams must adopt 'agile/lean' techniques. In this way teams can 'create' the extra time and resource that clearly most Employers and Consultants seek.

The issues of competitive procurement are discussed elsewhere, but it is felt that 'lack of resources', although a real problem to those noting this issue, is in the total project context, somewhat illusionary. Accepting a level of standardisation and adopting a 'right first time' principle has the capacity to release later resources frequently spent in reworking (quoted as up to 30 per cent (Graves, *Building*, 27 February 1998)). It is suggested, therefore, that both Employer and Consultant may achieve longer term efficiencies by considering in greater depth the basis upon which the initial brief and design is based. The previous examples of Wal-Mart, Amec Construction and McDonalds in Chapter 7 are all based on clarity of goals, roles and motivation. The methods and indeed the results may not be palatable to all, but the strategic focus towards a stated outcome must be commended.

Timescales are frequently dictated by deadlines, either real or arbitrary, but

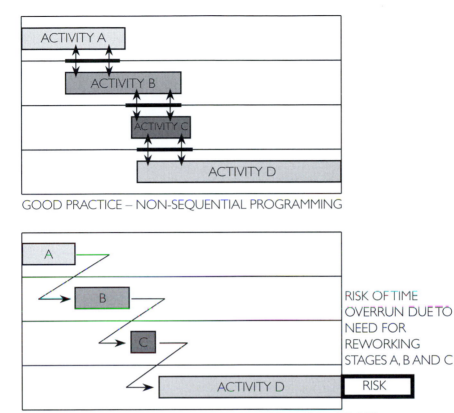

GOOD PRACTICE – NON-SEQUENTIAL PROGRAMMING

COMMON RESPONSE – LINEAR CONDENSED WORK STAGES

Figure 8.5 Comparison of response to 'fast-track'

the response is usually referenced to 'fast-track' systems. In practice, lack of time for appropriate response by Consultants was cited by many respondents to the survey, both Consultants themselves and Employers. So often 'fast-track' simply means 'compression'. The difference between 'real fast-track' and the popular interpretation is illustrated by Figure 8.5.

The simplistic view taken by NEDO in 1983, in their document *Faster Building for Industry* makes the flawed assumption that detail design or working drawings can fruitfully start before planning consent has been achieved. It may have been the case at that time but certainly the risks associated with such a strategy are significant. Strategies that allow for risk-free detail design need to be devised and these will relate to issues of standardisation, modularisation and prefabrication.

Crude compression of programmes carries a strong risk of a project performance gap developing, with a high risk of overrun. Non-sequential programming does offer the potential to 'create' time within a restricted timescale, but demands the careful management of the interfaces between activities if it is to be productive. It is also clear that advantages are finite; limits must be accepted to ensure that a compressed non-sequential model does not emerge.

The British Property Federation system superficially appears to be following a linear route that accords with tradition, however the subtlety of responsibilities, co-ordination techniques and changing responsibilities have alleged speed advantages. The concept of design team leaders, as opposed to managers, and the importance of the Client representative are key components of the system, if gains are to be achieved.

Comparisons with the car industry have been derided. This is quite correct insofar as the automotive product clearly benefits from a managed lead-in time, repetition, limited futures and the opportunity to build full-scale working mock-ups. At the design stage, however, all of the lessons learnt by the car industry can be applied to construction. The non-sequential nature of car design allows all Designers to work in parallel. This not only allows a more integrated total design but allows each individual Designer an appropriate timescale without extending the total design period. The realisation of this target demands, again, acceptance of goals, roles and motives. IT-based project knowledge hubs are integral to this process.

The briefing process

The widely quoted reason for failure is 'needs change during project'. As noted previously this would appear to be, in part, a euphemism for inadequately defined and considered initial requirements. It also appears to imply a brief and design, that by prescription and rigidity, cannot readily accommodate change. A reasonable presumption has been noted: 'Any organisation that requires a building is in a state of change.' It reinforces the inevitability of uncertainty and the inability of an Employer to 'cast in stone' requirements for the convenience of the design team.

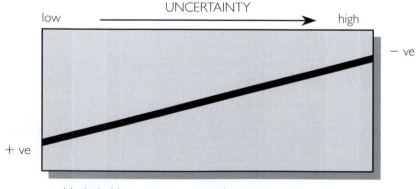

Undesirable outcomes – negative
Desirable outcomes – positive

Figure 8.6 Uncertainty versus outcomes

Maintaining the strategic relevance of the project is critical. Most projects will involve change to:

1   the business;
2   work practice;
3   work space.

Considerations of the strategic issues of the briefing process as defined in Chapter 3 and decision-making on a scale of reversibility–irreversibility (Nutt 1988, p. 130), would do much to reduce the criticality of this issue. The strategic consideration of undesirable and desirable outcomes supports the concepts of loose fit and phased briefing (See Figure 8.6). A reversal of the effort shown in Figure 5.17 is required to change the culture of 'instant solution', which increasingly means expensive and late.

In the context of space planning, case studies (McGregor and Shiem-Shin Then 1999, p. 58) have shown that so often due to alleged 'lead-in' times, furniture has been ordered before the space planning strategy and plan is in place. This instantly places a straight jacket on both Employer and design team, potentially resulting in inappropriate solutions.

Simple assumptions are made during the briefing process. The Employer must understand their own organisation if there is to be any opportunity to develop an appropriate information flow during the briefing process. The potential impertinence of a Consultant asking an Employer whether they indeed understand their own organisation should be tackled with some care! But Employers should ask themselves whether the person charged with liasing with Consultants and representing the organisation has a full overview of the whole organisation and its long-term objectives and motives.

Strategies for improvement in briefing cannot be 'pigeon holed'. It is an ongoing process, that ideally starts from demand identified by the business plan and ongoing post-occupancy evaluation, and continues throughout the life of the facility. In traditional and more everyday terms, the process is more often simply the information flow between Employer and Consultant in that short period known as the design process. In either extreme of the briefing concept, there are essentially four elements to the process that require active consideration:

1   roles of contributors;
2   structure of the process and the outcomes, both positive and negative;
3   management of the information flow and its conduits;
4   appropriateness of language.

The question of roles relates to all stakeholders of a project and demands appropriate empowerment.

Process structure is required to allow the appropriate consideration of the breadth and depth of all briefs. This study has emphasised the time, cost, function and aesthetic brief that are clearly major elements of a total project brief. But there are several other independent *and* interdependent briefs that also require addressing, for example:

- energy;
- environment;
- user;
- community;
- facility.

The facility brief is considered to be a bridge between the User and Employer, and between operational and strategic management. It is a key missing element of many ongoing processes and is considered in greater depth in the forthcoming section.

The management of the dynamic issues of the briefing process must demand clear and active input into issues such as:

- Team Dynamic – structure – knowledge/skills – synergy;
- Feedback – to team – to user – subsequent managers – all stakeholders;
- Loops – reappraisal – new knowledge – change to technology/work practice;
- Sequential Phasing – structured information flow and decision process.

These issues demand, specifically, that active conduits for feedback and review must be incorporated into all briefing processes. The short cut referred to in Figure 5.20 and reproduced here as Figure 8.7 for convenience, must be avoided. Similarly, the agenda of speed, or indeed the convenience of available information from Employers, should not divert attention from producing an incremental and phased approach to the briefing process. If strategic drift is to be avoided, then it is essential that key issues are addressed before the plethora of minor, but still potentially important issues, overwhelm the design team. In any project it is not unreasonable that the project briefing process as such will have the highest priority. This should not, however, be to the absolute detriment of the service brief between Employers and their design team.

The appropriate use of a two-way service brief, described later in this chapter, between the design team leader and the Employer should endeavour to clarify the need for the involvement of all stakeholders, within and outside of the organisation. Similarly, the same service agreement should ensure the retention of the Employers' involvement for the duration of the project.

The roles of consultants and employers

Roles and leadership

The survey shows that there is a clear difference of perception as to the timing of the Consultant's appointment and their contribution. It is suggested that this contributes to the difference of opinion, and also to the level of contribution that Consultants make to the briefing process. As noted by Allison (1997, p. 27), contributors to any given project will have a defined involvement life and few will be

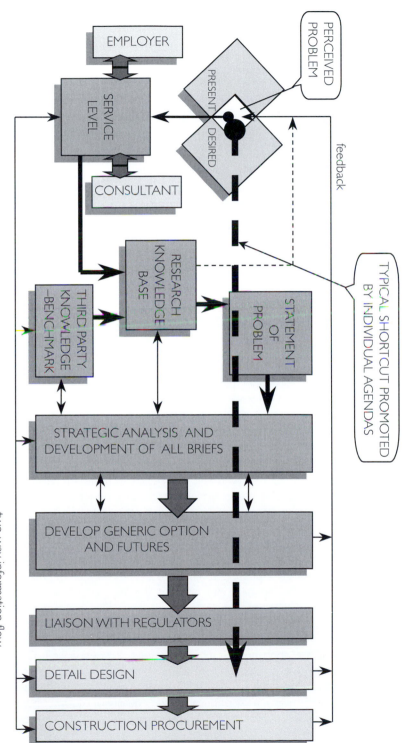

Figure 8.7 Briefing and design process shortcut (repeated)

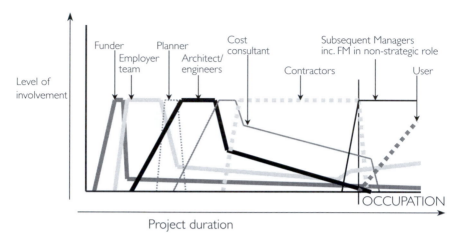

Traditional procurement with segmented roles

Figure 8.8 Changing levels of involvement and contribution

involved from inception to completion. Figure 8.8 illustrates the typical duration of levels of input for various contributors to any given stage of a project. Additionally the project cycle sees changes to the level of interest and power as well as simple 'involvement'. Figure 8.9 indicates this shift in the situation of a typical office for a User Employer, and funded by an Institution.

In common with other contributors the position of the Consultants moves during the project cycle. The particular concern, however, of most Employers in practice is with the level of perceived service and role. Expectation of Consultants' services must be seen directly in relationship to their terms of reference. Using the RIBA term of appointment as a model which reflects those of other professional associations, it can be observed that services are seen as compartmentalised packages to be provided at predetermined stages of a project. In reality few projects follow the neat sequential path indicated by the RIBA work plan and form of appointment.

Current practice encourages a single project leader, either project manager or Architect, for the project duration, citing consistency and continuity as favoured advantages. While it is possible to envisage an all-encompassing management over Figure 8.8, this fails to take into account the logic of using special skills when appropriate, and suggests a multi-skilled superman. The concept of a virtual team leader consisting of all parties, each having a maximum influence at any one time, has the benefit of ensuring that the most appropriate skilled person is leader of the team at the appropriate time ('the wheel of dominance'). Continuity is, of course, critical and the concept of a changing leader is only possible if project knowledge can be open to all. The IT-based project hub at this point becomes indispensable. Similarly, unity of purpose and equality of motivation are essential.

Government sponsored departments have in recent years created the term 'deliverables' as a term which is intended to engender 'firm purpose', clear goals and an objective commercial approach. These are commendable attributes and it

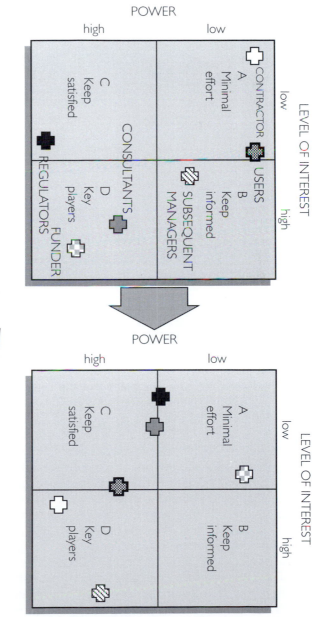

Figure 8.9 Stakeholder mapping

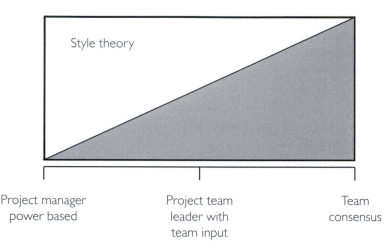

Figure 8.10 The range of leadership

is important for all parties to understand the ultimate results and elements to be produced, but it is suggested that this focus on 'deliverables' avoids consideration of how they are to be achieved.

From this study it is clear that many Employers consider that it is the way in which design and Consultancy services are provided that frequently leads to the gap of expectation/realisation. Issues of leadership style become relevant, as the means to create an appropriate culture is sought to allow an improved balance between the 'what' and the 'how'. The spectrum of options are shown in Figure 8.10.

It has been noted several times that the construction industry frequently blames Employers for project performance gaps. It seems inappropriate that both Consultants and Contractors, who are setting out to act as a service industry and provide a service to an Employer, should criticise the Employers' inability to perform. As a service provider it would appear to be more appropriate that the industry should provide expert and structured guidance that will *enable* Employers to perform. A key proposal for closing the performance gap within briefing must be the empowerment of the Employer. Providing the means and methodology for appropriate Client involvement should be a key part of any improvement strategy.

It has been noted (Barrett and Stanley 1999, p. 30) that Clients should 'understand the basis of the construction process'. Certainly if this is possible then it provides a common platform for the development of a scheme, language and brief. Too often, however, Employers are absorbed with their own business and really have little interest in the mechanical process of design and construction. For many there is a parallel to purchasing a car. What is important is that the customer (Employer) has a fair and reasonable expectation of performance, cost and delivery date of the car. The motor industry is significantly assisted by high quality brochures, fully working demonstration vehicles and an entire magazine industry dedicated to testing, describing and comparing competitors. It may be a different industry, but for those Clients wishing to avoid detailed knowledge of the construction industry it would seem to offer lessons.

Egan noted (*Architects Journal*, 3 February 2000, p. 38) that 'nobody is prepared to take responsibility for satisfying the Client'. The traditional divided role, he believed, left Clients to their own devices in considering which 'team' member was the most appropriate to manage.

The differentiation between design management and design leadership has received much recent attention. The Tavistock Institute (1999), in an initial draft consultation paper, has suggested that up to the traditional RIBA stage E the Architect is best placed to integrate (lead) the design team, but that perhaps others are better placed to manage. The management is described as 'dealing with those administrative issues that some Consultants have found unappealing', and consequently are often neglected. The same draft consultative paper considers that Contractors are preferred as Managers after stage E when 'design independencies' are resolved by the Architect.

Methodologies need to be developed within the briefing process to capture the 'values' of a project. Draft responses (The Tavistock Institute 1999) to the government concerning architects and the integrated supply chain consider that the Architect has a central role in assisting Clients to formulate and clarify these 'values'. They further conclude that, fundamentally, 'design process' is required to retain and develop the 'kernel' of the initial design. Their conclusions concur with those of others and of the Author's 1998 research, noting four steps for the achievement of improvement in this area:

1   Architects (with other Consultants) are to be involved at the conception of a brief and with Users at an early stage.
2   A complete team of designers and Consultants is to be assembled at the earliest opportunity.
3   The whole design team is to be involved with suppliers and contractors from the earliest opportunity.
4   All are to be agreed on a common goal and possess acceptable and visible motivation.

It has been suggested (Saxon, *Architects Journal*, 3 February 2000, p. 38) that prime contracting and improved Design and Build will mark the end of the tradition of employing an Architect separately and directly. Cynically, one could report that as long as it is customary for Architects to give so much for so little as they attempt to secure a commission, they will indeed be in demand. This is not an endorsement of this style of business. Taking the opinion of others, that direct appointments may become less popular, however, it can be seen that it will become more necessary for them (Architects and indeed any Consultant) to create 'value'. This will still demand direct dialogue with Employers and users. It can be seen that rather than being marginalised, Architects have the potential to contribute significantly more to a project, by becoming involved in project definition, brief making, value management, research and development and post-occupancy analysis. This is of course at the expense of such detail involvement with the later stages of

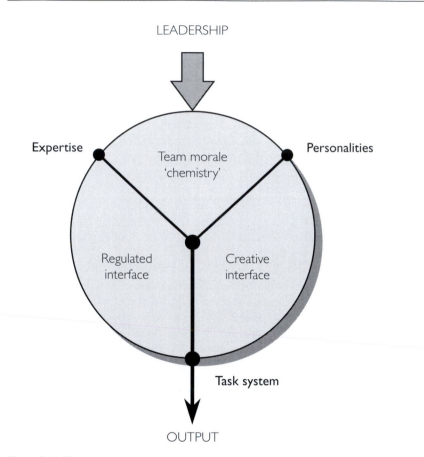

LEADERSHIP

Expertise

Personalities

Team morale
'chemistry'

Regulated
interface

Creative
interface

Task system

OUTPUT

Figure 8.11 The team and the task system

procurement. It demands, however, an FM style thinking, if meaningful dialogue having any value for these issues, is to be achieved.

An ongoing debate is continuing regarding the roles of the different contributors to the design and procurement of a project, for example, who should lead the team, and who is best qualified. There are so called critical comments regarding the inadequacies and failures of contributors whether Architects, quantity surveyors, Contractors, project managers. The words written on this subject over the years would probably fill several stacks of a library; they all miss the point however. All of the skills are relevant and necessary. Every reader will have seen a building 'designed' by a Builder, Quantity Surveyor or Facility Manager, and similarly will probably have seen a set of 'un-buildable' working drawings from an Engineer or Architect. This is not a basis upon which to deny the relevance of any of the parties referred to above. It is clear that a formula is required that respects and accepts that at different stages of a project, different skills are necessary.

All projects need to develop a task system (Figure 8.11) which is capable of managing the variety of expertise and personality that will invariably be evident. Acceptance of the need, and indeed desirability, for both a creative and a regula-

Figure 8.12 The Employer's foreground role

tory interface is a significant step towards a focused team synergy. The appropriateness of leadership and team style is dependant upon the nature of the team and the project itself, but the common link in all projects is the Employer.

Two-way service agreements and the role of the employer

There is an accepted correlation between success and the level of input, notably by the Employer, at the early stages of a project. Experienced Employers with dedicated and focused professional resources, and the inexperienced with 'months of pre-planning', endorse this view. Following the latter, and the views contained in much literature, it would appear incumbent upon any Employer with specific expectations to maintain an influence throughout the project. Figure 8.12, illustrates the 'foreground role' that must be adopted to maintain consistency of purpose and continued transparency of the direct interface with all contributors. Abdication of this role carries risk.

The evidence of consistently good briefing between Employer and Consultant is somewhat 'thin'. Both parties do, however, clearly struggle with issues arising from the absence of suitable agreements. It is considered that the briefing of Consultants should be a two-way exercise between Employer and Consultant. It should also range beyond the agreement of 'deliverables' and consider the 'how and why' (see Figure 8.13).

A neglected element in this two-way exercise is the definition of the Employer's 'foreground role'. All too frequently the single point of contact can become little more than a postbox (despite recommendations to the contrary, see Chapter 4), dealing with the project as an administrative exercise. The 'sign off' of drawings does not imply understanding by those expected to 'sign', and can merely be an extension of a QA type system.

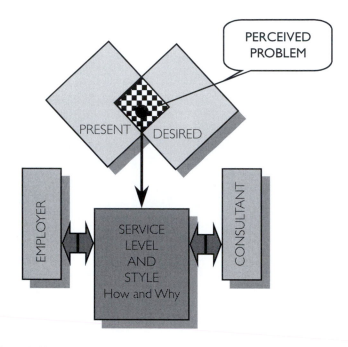

Figure 8.13 Two-way service agreement

BAA have adopted many of the 'partnership' arrangements referred to by Rover and McDonalds, but also have a particular emphasis on the selection of Consultants. It is now formalised so as to use the EC Journal format with clear service briefs. This offers the opportunity to appoint the most appropriate Consultant and, further, to explore the real demands of service required. For success, however, such a strategy must be an irregular activity as it is a fundamental part of partnering that some continuity is provided; open competition on a project-by-project basis must be avoided.

The concept of the two-way service agreement simply involves: How, what, when and why. It is essential that both Employer and Consultant are 'as one' with the agreement, and how each of the four issues are to be addressed. It is essential that values are prioritised and scenarios agreed to deal with demand for design development, change and evaluation.

The proforma in Figure 8.14 suggests the type of arrangement that may be agreed 'up front' before the project itself is considered. The range of projects, relationships and organisations means that one single two-way agreement cannot be universal. The proforma is intended as a guide to both Employers and Consultants as to the range of issues that should be addressed at the outset, specifically ranging beyond the simple 'deliverables'. It would be expected that organisations may adapt and expand the model, for it is certainly not exhaustive.

This is a learning process without which projects embark upon shaky foundations. It should not be assumed that a long-term repetitive relationship with an organisation means that this becomes irrelevant. How many Employers and

SERVICE BRIEF

EMPLOYER INPUT	CRITICAL ISSUES	CONSULTANT INPUT
Essential outcomes Unacceptable outcomes	CRITICAL ISSUES	Success factors
Site information Financial arrangements Conditions of 'deal' Access to organisation Provision of resources	DELIVERABLES	Presentation package Specification Programme Cost plan Drawings
Industry standards Organisation standards	QUALITY / TOLERANCE	BS/ISO In-house systems
Structure of communication Suitable contact Continuity of decision Timely issue Transparency/honesty Levels of authority Methods of communication Assessment of knowledge	SERVICE DELIVERY	Interface with all third parties Method of communication Transparency/honesty Continuity of personnel Timely issue Cultural fit Agreed motivator
Internal management Process input	TEAMWORK	Project management Design team leadership Internal communication and review
Input to user/organisation Value engineering Timely assessment of options Agreement of limit of development Research – process and user	RESOURCING	Size and quality of team Research Defined parameters of design development Specialist inputs
Cash flow Budget clarity	FINANCE	Cashflow Profit target Cost versus resources

Figure 8.14 Two-way service agreement – a prompt

Consultants have drifted into relationships, and despite presumably satisfactory project outcomes, consistently find the same annoying non-productive issues arising. Adopting a two-way service agreement now will demonstrate commitment to learning and improvement for mutual benefit.

Communication and media

As professionals and Employers concentrate on core business the communication gulf can only have the potential to widen. The management of the internal and external interfaces shown by Figure 8.1, are essential and increasingly critical.

The issues of language, lay user appreciation and media are fundamental. Communication was cited by 25 per cent of all Employers as a basic reason for failure in 1989; this remains the primary underlying issue throughout the author's study and many others. As noted previously, culture, education and experience all colour perception. Written words can contain ambiguity, drawings may simply be an alien media, and models often give seductive 'man on the moon' views.

The symbolic content of graphics style, text and form will have a certain effect upon the beholder, which may assist, alienate or dumbfound. Current references to the 'sexy image', 'the narrative' and 'storyboard' demonstrate the move from the standard plan and elevation, which is wholly unacceptable for most Employers.

Information technology, specifically virtual reality (VR), is often quoted as the way forward: 'the ultimate opportunity to walk through your facility before a brick is laid'. VR, either static or video, is of major assistance to both Consultant and Employer, but current available technology lacks any tactile quality and may be used to great effect in gaining approval of designs which subsequently appear somewhat more mundane.

Secure understanding requires touching and seeing at first hand. Expansion of the Building Centre concept in 'set' format may offer better opportunities to readily appreciate products and materials in situ as opposed to designers' sample boards. It is suggested that, as the industry achieves a greater level of standardisation (in whatever form), this becomes more feasible and may be developed to provide spatial models at full size allowing people to consider work spaces and fittings, without the cost of producing mock-ups for their individual one-off project.

The sensory element of design must not be ignored. The 'you are there' experience is essential to ensure that there will be no surprises. The need to get the Client on board and avoidance of the 'fait accompli' presentation is critical. Production of storyboards with combinations of photo montages, drawings and text has proved effective. The invitation to the Client to produce his own storyboard using paste-up photographs from magazines, for example, is becoming commonplace. The use of montages and photographs of existing work by other Designers should not be feared by Consultants. Again, it has proved to be a very efficient way of understanding the values and aspirations of any particular Employer. It satisfies the demands of an Employer wishing to make fast progress and satisfies the Consultant in the avoidance of countless abortive computer models and sketches. Optimal effort by Designers and Employers can quickly allow them to 'come together' in terms of aspirations and the setting of values. Cook of BDP (Porter 2000, p. 52) sees their communication process as developing and selling a design narrative. The narrative demands a wide range of techniques as appropriate for a wide range of Clients. The integration of IT and multimedia alongside traditional touch and feel boards is considered essential.

Knowing the Client and, again, establishing the 'how' before the 'what', allows the process to be both profitable and 'painless' for all involved.

The simple decisions in terms of communication and visualisation techniques can be far-reaching. The clear multi-coloured image on the CAD computer screen rarely retains such clarity by the time it has been plotted and copied, invariably in black and white. The Employer (and later the Contractor) struggles as the CAD author often remains blissfully unaware. The lack of an appreciation loop gives no opportunity for improvement. Similarly, innovative presentation techniques designed to impress peers, such as the currently popular 'worm's eye' view may be superficially attractive, but does not aid the communication process! (Again the old Chinese proverb seems quite appropriate, – '100 tellings is not as good as one seeing'.)

More dynamic and honest techniques must be agreed between the Employer and the Consultant, that allow the expertise of the relevant Consultant to be fully exploited. Many Employers appear to pay professional fees and accept or request a technical service only. Conversely, professional Consultants frequently and willingly accept this status as an aid to their commercial agenda. The result is that Employers often fail to get the best from external Consultants, and the latter find themselves struggling with conflicting and poorly developed requirements.

The role of facility management

Role and contributing skills

The BIFM survey of 1999 demonstrates that there are some 30 separate categories of activity undertaken by facility managers as a body. The managers themselves are represented by a dozen professions and some 18 qualifications. It is not surprising, therefore, that there is some confusion regarding the role of facility management and where it may fall within the design process. Furthermore, facility management may be part of the Employer organisation or an external consultancy. In practice, the use of facility management in either context has a low profile. Acknowledgement of the issues raised by facility management such as sustainability, life costing and the space budget is evident; but the short-term horizons of most Employer groups is somewhat contrary. In many organisations this is supplemented by significant guilt, as acknowledgement of FM is followed with little action. With the exception of a few enlightened Employers, the concept of an FM brief/policy is rather rare. As referenced previously, it was with some embarrassment that one significant Employer, with a BIFM Certificate on the adjacent wall, admitted that the company had no facility management policy at all.

The 1999 BIFM survey confirmed much of the author's perception that FM is misunderstood and is still considered by a number of people to be an 'unavoidable evil'. The tide is changing, however, and it is noted that 58 per cent of Employers believe FM has high or medium strategic importance within their organisation. It is disappointing therefore that the facility management brief within projects is rarely developed. Despite much discussion concerning issues of user

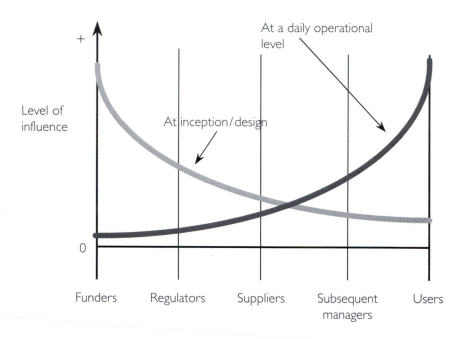

Figure 8.15 The gulf to be bridged

satisfaction, adaptability, space, energy and life cost, the recent focus of project success has revolved around project management.

In practice, there remains a vast gulf between initial instigators and ultimate users. Attempts to bring together users to participate are of restricted value. Frequently the interface between Employer and the design team falls between an Employer's representative and design team leader. The former is frequently inexpert and struggling with their core function. The latter often lacks any in-depth knowledge of the Client organisation and is struggling with time and cost agendas for their own organisation and the project. Figure 8.15 illustrates the gulf between various stakeholders that is evident in practice. It is proposed that facility management is appropriately positioned to bridge this gap which appears unlikely to close, due to the many diverse agendas discussed previously.

As long ago as 1934 (Lord Alfred Bossom quoted by Cain in 'Building Down Barriers', *Faculty of Building Journal*, February 1999), it was pointed out that poor building layout added to production cost (15 per cent in the case of the manufacture of cotton goods, for example), yet the relationship between building design and function so often remains tenuous. Although such problems may easily, and perhaps correctly, be dismissed as issues of communication, the consequences still remain unresolved. The project cycle sees shifts in the positioning of all project stakeholders in terms of 'power versus interest'. For as long as this is maintained, the resolution of real communication issues remains elusive.

The role of facility management as a bridge builder or translator holds great potential. The gap between instigators and ultimate users can be filled by facility management's informed understanding of the organisational process, but without

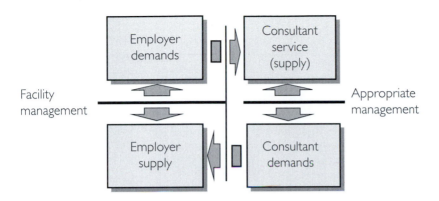

Figure 8.16 The interfaces with and within the Employer

the preconceptions and hidden agendas frequently carried by Employers, design teams and Contractors alike. A bridge between inception and design requires the management of the interface between Consultant and Employer, and *within* Employer, to provide a balanced response to the issue of supply and demand, as illustrated in Figure 8.16. FM has an ability to provide a pivotal role, as Spedding (1994, p. 76) notes: 'The FM role is to integrate user interests (demand) with the building team (supply)'. It also has the skills to take a holistic overview and manage the 'quality budget'.

It is suggested that there has been an over-emphasis of the time/cost budgets and this has contributed to increased failure of elements of the quality brief. Clearly, from this and other studies the time/finance briefs are critical, but this should not be to the exclusion of other issues. The view (Preiser 1993, p. 338) that facility planning is at the core of the strategic brief is slowly gaining exposure as PFI build-ing projects are developing an FM design element, as discussed previously.

It is evident that many organisations see facility management as an opera-tional exercise; the strategic skills available to this profession are not appreciated and wider exposure of these skills is needed. These skills must be integrated into the design team to provide adequate representation of the space budget, total life design and future organisational strategies. Acknowledged deficiencies in know-ledge management, building performance and post-occupancy evaluation are clearly the domain of facility management.

In the same way that the Employer has a 'foreground role' (Figure 8.12) to perform in the project team, it is proposed that facility management has a 'reflected role' across the same breadth and in parallel. Figure 8.17 completes the rectangle, allowing a holistic input into each contributor and providing opportunity for a consistent interface with the Employer.

The FM brief

In recent years the profiles of briefs such as health and safety, energy and accessi-bility have steadily increased. The driver has in the main been legislative, driven in

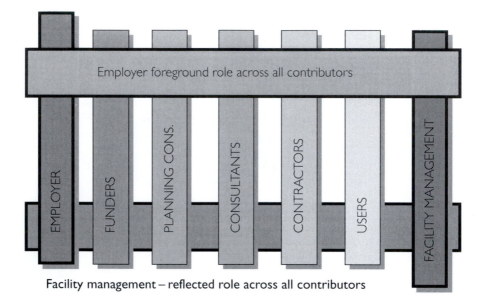

Facility management – reflected role across all contributors

Figure 8.17 A reflected role for FM

turn partly by a moral conscience. Issues such as quality, environment and whole life design are now beginning to increase their profile.

Quality, in terms of space, comfort and support services, is driven by rising user expectations and demands from organisations as they concentrate on their core business. Environmental issues have similar drivers but, additionally, global and local conscience and legislation are being strengthened. Considerations of whole life design embodies all of the above drivers, and as a consequence an effect is being seen throughout industry. Similarly concepts of 'lean/agile thinking' in the broadest context will make change in building design inevitable. The increased profile of these issues can only instigate a rise in the status and profile of the Facility Management brief (see Figure 8.18). The generally cited reason for failure to formalise such a brief, namely, lack of resource, was frequently applied to health and safety, energy and accessibility. With sufficient demand and proven benefit, however, it can be seen that such barriers disappear.

The integration of facility management within the team as a strategic resource, not simply a 'bolt-on fixer', is fundamental to any serious attempt to close the gap between expectation and realisation. The growth of risk assessment and value engineering has been Quantity Surveyor and construction led. There is, however, little evidence of 'use engineering', despite the protestations of many Employers that they are indeed seeking holistic improvement. Many Clients have begun to appreciate the potential that strategic facility management can provide within their organisation, but few have acted upon this view.

Acknowledged failures in the areas of cost and time have encouraged management responses in the form of clear identifiable project control systems. Attempts to improve functional and qualitative issues have generally resulted in

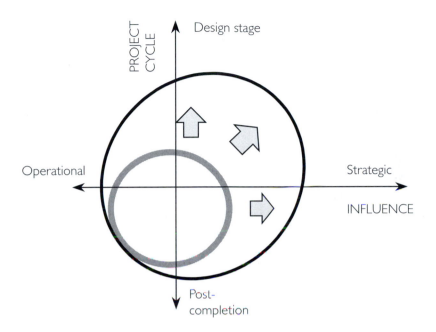

Figure 8.18 Future directions for FM

more communication, but unfortunately without the anticipated improvement in understanding. The FM brief remains underdeveloped. A primary reason would appear to be the lack of any acknowledged model for this brief. The role of facility management has developed rapidly to the extent that it has become 'all things to all men'. Employer perception ranges from 'janitorial services' to strategic property asset management.

Traditional singular professions, such as architects and surveyors, have little knowledge of FM. The majority believe that FM issues have little impact on their Clients, their service or the design project as a whole. Responses are, however, polarising. Although many singular Consultants are concerned that another member within a design team will further marginalise their personal role, there are those who are embracing FM. Cynically, it could be argued that these Consultants are 'going with the flow', but most reasonably respond that the FM approach provides for the genuine resolution of many long-standing issues. Facility management is, within the design process, as much an approach as it is a discrete profession. Indeed it has been referred to as a 'profession of professionals'.

The range of activity that appears to be undertaken under the umbrella of facility management is extensive, as evidenced by the BIFM (1999) survey. It is clear, however, that in a design context many of these subsequent management or hotel activities are directly influenced by the hardware of the physical design. The obvious reconciliation of 'space to need' is an immediate strategic input by facility management into design, but clearly the ancillary items will, if they have no input, become the major headaches of tomorrow. The model in Figure 8.19 shows the 'supply and demand' model as a framework for a facility brief.

SUPPLY ← ——————————————— → DEMAND

REAL ESTATE AND BUILDING CONSTRUCTION	BUILDING OPERATIONS AND MAINTENANCE	FACILITY PLANNING	GENERAL/OFFICE SERVICES
Strategic	Tactical	Strategic	Tactical
Hardware		Software	
Provides sites and buildings, fit-outs and adaptations, operations and maintenance of buildings		Allocation of space, services and equipment to meet management objectives and user through time	

• New building design and construction management • Acquisition and disposal of sites and buildings • Negotiation and management of leases • Advice on property matters • Control of capital budgets LANDLORD ACTIVITIES • Assignment and sub-letting • Promotion/market support	• Run and maintain plant • Maintain building fabric • Manage and undertake adaptation • Energy management • Security • Voice and data communication • Control of operating budget • Monitor performance • Supervise cleaning and decoration	• Strategic space planning • Set corporate planning standards and guidelines • Identify user needs • Space planning – workspace • Monitor space use • Select and control of workspace equipment • Define performance measures • Computer aided facility management (CAFM)	• Provide and manage support services • Office purchasing (consumables and equipment) • Non-building contract services (catering, travel etc.) • Reprographic services • Housekeeping services SUB-LET SERVICES • Multi-tenant services • Administration co-ordination

Figure 8.19 The supply and demand model of FM (UCL 1997)

The facility brief is supplemental to the design brief, to the aesthetic brief and the finance brief, but has the potential to provide an integrating element and to fill in much of the 'interspace'. The danger of producing check lists and rigid documentation has been described at length. For this reason it is not considered appropriate to produce a format for this elusive FM brief. Figure 8.20, however, demonstrates the range of impinging issues that need to be fed into the design process. Development of an acknowledged model facility brief has the potential to clarify the role of FM, and demonstrate the benefits that FM can bring to the design process and all involved with it. A contributor's power and influence at a particular stage of a project is not always appropriate to the level of interest or potential contribution. This is particularly evident in the FM arena.

Discussion (Trickett, *Architects Journal*, 7 October 1999, p. 37) has turned to the value of designers and in particular Architects, but management is seen to be equal in relation to design, in terms of the effects exerted upon users. The consideration of the physical environment in terms of hardware, and management in terms of software, is the realm of facility management. For Designers, the challenge of being closer to Employers and becoming part of organisational change, is FM thinking within design context. The preservation of the delicate balance between the many complex issues during change is a skill that requires thinking beyond pure design, and indeed beyond pure management.

It is clear that no one profession has the ability to reconcile all of the conflicting demands that inevitably arise during the life of the project, but the inclusion of FM as an equal member of the design team can act as a glue to hold together

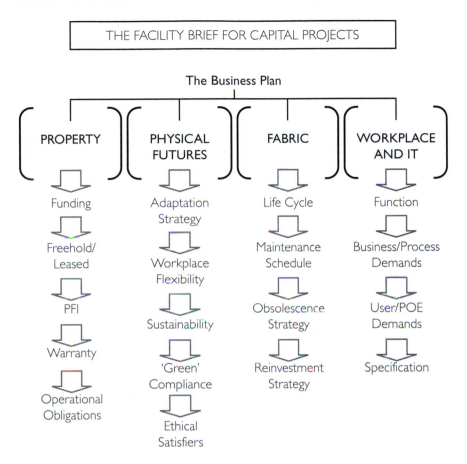

Figure 8.20 The start of a facilities brief

the matrix of professions involved. The payback for the team is clear. Facility management has the potential to close the gap between expectation and realisation.

Future strategies

Six strategies are suggested as a means to improve current practice. Some warrant significant development and investment, whereas others reiterate good practice that rarely seems to occur, but may be instigated immediately.

I. Two-way briefing for roles and service expectations

To redress the balance of 'how' as opposed to 'what', it is proposed that service agreements such as the RIBA work plan/appointment should be disbanded or modified to allow for and provoke Client and Consultant into a meaningful discussion regarding their respective roles. An agreement that sets out the expectations of Client services in addition to those of the Consultant will focus attention on project team needs and avoid gaps in expected service and support for all contributors. Initially the agreement of the status of the project, upon the involvement of any Consultant, would immediately remove one of the barriers to understanding and service observed in the survey. The adoption of 'role' presentations by each contributor at key project stages will further ensure a mutual clarity of purpose. The empowerment of the Employer, the agreement on boundaries of authority and acceptance of the Employer's foreground role will ensure appropriate and meaningful communication at all stages of the process.

Reference

Figure 8.14 Two-way service agreement –a prompt
Figure 8.12 The Employer's foreground role

2. Knowledge base

The establishment of readily and easily accessible knowledge bases are fundamental to the development of efficient and zero-based briefing techniques. Current ad hoc databases are inadequate. Facility management has a central role in the provision of Employers' property databases incorporating POEs, utilisation, whole life costs etc.

    The five steps to knowledge management can be instigated in all organisations to improve or consolidate existing systems:

Identification – Retention – Conversion – Distribution – Utilisation.

    Project knowledge hubs are a natural development of good knowledge management. Following the six stages previously described, single project hubs can be instigated immediately, after which multiple hubs can be developed. The goal is for hubs to encompass first one organisation and project, and then ultimately through to a 'partnered' team and multiple projects.

    The provision of national and international accessibility to building and design data demands a government or industry wide forum. This has been alluded to in the Egan report, and warrants significant investigation and investment if goals are to be achieved. The level of support offered by publicly available knowledge bases is expanding rapidly, and must be harnessed and utilised.

    The excessive dependence on 'last year's experience' by Employers and Consultants is a culture of stagnation that must be reversed.

Reference

Figure 8.4 Learning between projects

3. Multiple project leaders

The arguments for continuity and retention of a single project leader will recede as project knowledge hubs become common practice. As observed by many survey respondents, there is no one profession 'as a right' permitted to lead. Concentration on relevant key issues and consequent improvement of service and efficiency may be encouraged by use of appropriate project leaders for the given stage.

Successful implementation demands improved leadership and management training amongst all involved with the project, and establishment of accessible project knowledge hubs. The 'virtual team' leader concept requires the Employer's foreground role, a mutual respect for a variety of skills and an open approach to project knowledge. Unity of purpose and motivation are essential.

Leadership style in the multiple model will, by default, be consensus-based. The harnessing of the team dynamic and potential synergy require the creation of a project specific task system, which must include every individual involved with the project.

References

Figure 8.8 Changing levels of involvement and contribution
Figure 8.11 The team and the task system

4. Project brief – flexibility and feedback

The overall project briefing process consists of a variety of elemental briefs, four of which have formed the basis of this study.

Both Employers and Consultants need to see this in the form of an ongoing two-way information flow. The adoption of a phased briefing demands discipline by Consultant and Employer alike to avoid premature design and solution seeking that leads to rigidity. Avoidance of compartmentalised 'briefing stages' is the key to the development of appropriate solutions with a relevant priority being allocated to all requirements. The abandonment of sequential linear processes requires training and appreciation by all involved.

Feedback techniques, in either direction, warrant special consideration. User input, appropriately weighted, must be accepted and then users informed of a considered and balanced outcome rather than a disappointing 'fait accompli' on completion. Mere involvement is not sufficient, real understanding must be achieved.

The strengths and weaknesses of various media has been discussed; all are relevant, but with an increased emphasis on the use of the storyboard and exposure to 'real' examples in Building Centre sets, for key elements.

Reference

Figure 8.7 Briefing and design process shortcut

5. *The facility brief*

As part of any project brief, the development of a facility management brief is considered fundamental to the satisfying of organisational, operational and environmental demands. The issues of expectation and legislation, as noted, may drive this brief; however it is incumbent upon Consultants to demand its inclusion. A properly considered FM brief and input will significantly reduce the occurrence of many of the expectation–realisation gaps observed in the study.

The adoption of the proposed skeletal form of FM brief can start to close the gap between the physical product and the demands of Users, subsequent managers and business needs, etc.

Reference

Figure 8.20 The start of a facilities brief

6. *Resource allocation*

Current practice is encouraging shorter time periods for the development of Employer requirements and initial design. This simplistic trend must be halted if satisfaction levels are to be improved. Avoidance of strategic issues and the concentration on the 'instant' solution are practices that should be discarded.

Arguments of commercial pressure, by Employer and Consultant, preventing additional time up front, are flawed. Acknowledged reworking and change costs in the later stages of projects, *if avoided*, will fund better time and resources at the earlier stages.

Adoption of 'agile' and 'lean' thinking concepts should be a priority to maximise the effectiveness of limited resources. Focus attention and time on the critical success factors of the project. Welcome and direct the design input from product suppliers and manufacturers.

Phased briefing, referred to previously, will also assist by avoiding premature and time-consuming detail at the stage where strategic issues and adaptable proposals should be priority. The development of multi-layered briefs and the use of corresponding procurement strategies should be adopted to maximise the project team resource.

The adoption of project hubs, phased briefing and a clear team structure will allow the mutual agreement of key goals and non-sequential work. Establish a project methodology for parallel and non-sequential working as opposed to 'common practice compression' of traditional work stages.

Reference

Figure 8.5 Comparison of 'response' to 'fast-track'

The six strategies are relevant to any building project and remain relevant regardless of the construction procurement route. Each reflects the concerns and deficiencies in practice evident from the survey responses and subsequent interviews.

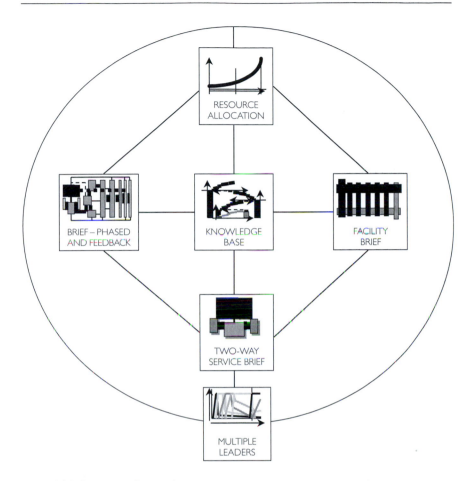

Figure 8.21 Summary of strategies

Figure 8.21 graphically summarises the strategies and refers to each by virtue of an icon back to previous discussion.

Concluding thoughts

Improvement strategies are fine but, much like the rash of Egan spawned initiatives, they hold little value if they are not implemented and utilised.

Selling the concept of holistic improvement is still a struggle. Last year's methods are always easy to replicate. Some may acknowledge the potential for improvement, but cynically observe that the initiatives are not 'rocket science' and therefore are somehow not worth pursuing. As a means of assisting the promotion of improvement techniques, large or small, Figure 8.22, shows a range of practice, from the lowest expectation to the highest. The purpose is to encourage the reader to superimpose a graph line reflecting their organisation's 'normal'

Two-way service agreement	Bespoke investigation and dedicated research	'Live' with the organisation and cyclical dialogue	Regular team with common goals, motives and structure	Two-way story boards, 3D, video, models, touchboards	Sequential incremental development with feedback loops	Early involvement of suppliers/conts with open book and motivators
Definitive set of roles, tasks and deliverables	Specialist sources of published data	Ongoing dialogue with all stakeholders	Regular team with individual agendas	Photo montage story boards, 3D CAD and sketches	Phased incremental linear development	Early involvement of negotiated suppliers/conts
RIBA / RICS etc.	Available IT or written sources	Dialogue with a range of management personnel	New team with external PM leadership	Photo realistic 3D CAD	Development to client / designer agenda	Early involvement of competitive contractors
Letter	Sought out experience	Prepare brief document /data sheet from client 'PM'	New team but with clear visible briefs	2 and 3D sketches with atmosphere	Production to a construction / qs programme	Competitive tender with shared motivators
Phone call	Available Experience	Accept client reps written / verbal 'wish list'	'Thrown' together by client with secret briefs	Traditional 2D line drawings	Unco-ordinated and unstructured detail design	One-off single stage competitive tender
SERVICE AGREEMENT	RESEARCH	BRIEFING PROCESS	TEAM STRUCTURE	DESIGN LANGUAGE	DESIGN PROCESS	PROCURE BUILDING

Figure 8.22 The score board

practice. Few will insert a straight line through all categories of 'minimal practice' and, conversely, few will indicate a straight line through all categories of 'best practice'. Particularly as previously noted, 'best ' practice in reality refers to a range of appropriate 'good' practices. Figure 8.22, or an adaptation, honestly completed, can be a powerful tool to encourage debate and improved practice within a team, whether internal or multi-organisational. Completion of 'the score board' in the mid-ranges is to be expected, based upon current 'normal' practice, but the aim must be to consistently *and appropriately* 'move the line up'.

Clearly, practical effort must be applied to the development and improvement of knowledge management at all levels, and this will involve a significant timeframe and investment. But there are no reasons why the next single project cannot adopt systems to capture, retain and disperse the knowledge base that will inevitably develop. Technology may help but it is the cultural shift that can happen immediately.

Other strategies, such as two-way service briefing, flexible and phased project briefing with feedback, and appropriate resource allocation can already be seen in 'best' practice, but fail to win recognition widely. Such proposals require like-minded parties to reap immediate benefits.

The lack of definition of the scope and form of the facility brief, has failed to persuade Employers of the benefits of an FM approach. The proforma produced as Figure 8.20 is however, a starting point. Acceptance of the project team as a learning forum, should not therefore inhibit immediate development of a project specific FM brief.

Disappointingly, the primary generic areas of project failure identified in the mid-1980s by Thamain and Wileman, and others, are reinforced by this study, and remain sufficiently topical to form the basis of the latest government reports and a plethora of 'good practice' documents.

Stumbling blocks remain to Egan's ideals, despite acknowledged benefits. Indeed research by the University of Bath in 1998 into the subject of 'partnering' revealed that a continuing lack of trust encourages a significant majority of Employers to choose Contractors on a contracted lowest price basis, shunning partnership arrangements, which are clearly a fundamental concept for Egan.

Fortunately changes in both business and global environments give hope that conditions now prevail to encourage positive improvement. Issues of quality, environment and customer focus, all supported by initiatives such as TQM, IIP, 'partnering' and PFI, gain profile. It is felt that subtle shifts in the attitudes of Consultants and Employers may lead to greater receptivity of ideas for the joint pursuit of improvement.

The emergence of facility management as a multi-skilled profession, acting beyond the operational, has the potential to develop as a translator at the interface of Employer and Design team. Becker (1991, p. 61) and Spedding (1994, p. 76) have both endorsed this view, and believe in the crucial role of the facility manager, referring to it as 'understanding consultants' and 'integrating supply and demand'. Facility management, as a 'profession of professionals', remains embryonic and requires a quantifiable track record, an accepted knowledge base and an appropriately perceived identity. Integration within the project design team from inception, and the development of an appropriate facility brief for each project, has the potential to reduce many of the expectation/realisation gaps observed in this study.

No one 'best' practice solution exists – appropriateness is the key. It is hoped that this study will have provoked some ideas for improvement and at least prompted the 'how' and 'why' questions that seem to have disappeared from much of everyday practice. Seen against the background of the 'impinging issues', the avoidance of repeated performance gaps can only be achieved by reducing the emphasis on the physical brief and the 'instant' solution culture. Improved performance requires a much broader interface than is evident in current practice.

This 'communication interface' is indeed the key to closing the gap between expectation and realisation. Communication between Employers and Consultants too often fails to address adequately both the relevance and quality of the information flow. As a consequence, assumption and presumption compound mutual misunderstanding of what are often already complex and dynamic issues.

References

Allinson, K. (1997) *Getting there by Design*, The Architectural Press, reprinted by Butterworth Heinman.

Atkin, Clarke and Smith (1996) *Benchmarking Best Practice Briefing and Design*, University of Salford, Construct IT Centre of Excellence.

Barrett, P. (1995a) *Facilities Management: Towards Best Practice*, Blackwell Science.

Barrett, P. (1993) *Profitable Practice for the Construction Professional*, E & FN Spon.

Barrett, P. (1995b) 'Quality Management for the Construction Professional – What a Mess!' *RICS Research Paper*, Vol. 1, No. 4, RICS.

Barrett, P. and Males, M. (1991) *Practice Management: New Perspectives for Construction Professionals*, E & FN Spon.

Barrett, P. and Stanley, C. (1999) *Better Construction Briefing*, Blackwell Science.

Bartlett (Bartlett School of Architecture) (1999) *Landscape of Change*, Ballast Wiltshier.

Becker, F. (1991) *The Total Workplace*, Van Nostrand Reinhold.

Bicknell, C. N. (1998) *Architectural Facilities Management*, MSc Report, University of Westminster, unpublished.

BIFM (1999) *Survey of Facilities Managers' Responsibilities*, BIFM.

Broh, R. A. (1982) *Managing Quality for Higher Profits*, McGraw Hill.

Brown, S. A. (1998) *Communication Interfaces*, MSc Report, UCL, unpublished.

Chessun, D. F. M. (1999) *The Interface between Project and Operational Management*, MSc Report, UCL, unpublished.

CIB (Construction Industry Board Working Group) (1997) *Briefing the Team*, Thomas Telford.

Cox, A. and Townsend, M. (1998) *Strategic Procurement in Construction*, Thomas Telford.

Cuff, D. (1996) *Architecture: The Story of Practice*, MIT Press.

Davenport, G. C. (1994) *Essential Psychology*, Collins Education.

DETR (1998–9) *Knowledge Management and IT in the Construction Industry*, Research Programme co-ordinated by D. Batholomew (forthcoming).

DETR (1998) *The Report of the Construction Industry Task Force: Rethinking Construction* (The Egan Report) HMSO.

Edwards, C. D. (1968) 'The Meaning of Quality', *Quality Progress*, October.

Franks, J. (1998) *Building Procurement Systems*, 3rd edition, Longman.

Garvin, D. (1988) *Managing Quality*, Harvard Business School, Free Press.

Gray, C., Hughes, W. and Bennet, J. (1994) *The Successful Management of Design*, The University of Reading Centre for Strategic Studies.

Gross, R. (1996) *Psychology*, Hodder and Stoughton.

Harrison, H. W. and Keeble, E. J. (1983) *Performance Specification for Whole Buildings: A Report on the BRE Studies 1974–1982*, Building Research Establishment.

Harwood, M. (1996) *Paper No. 2. The Management of Design Process in Architectural Practice*, Bartlett Research, University College, London.

Higgins, G. and Jessop, N. (1963) *Communications in the Building Industry*, Tavistock Publications.

Hill, J. (ed.) (1998) *Occupying Architecture: Between the Architect and the User*, Routledge.

HAPM (Housing Association Property Mutual Limited) (1991) *Defect Avoidance Manual – New Build*, Construction Audit.

Juran, T. (1974) *Quality Control Handbook*, McGraw Hill.

Juran, T. (1992) *Quality by Design*, Free Press.

Kernohan, D., Gray, J., Daish, J. and Joiner, D. (1996) *User Participation in Building Design and Management*, Butterworth Architecture.

Latham, Sir M. (1994) *Constructing the Team*, Government Report, HMSO.

Lehtinen, U. and Lehtinen, J. (1991) 'Two Approaches to service Quality Dimension, *The Services Industries Journal*, Vol. 11.

Lock, D. (1992) *Project Management*, Gower Publishing.

Lupton, S. and Stellakis, M. (1995) *Performance Specification, An Analysis of Trends and Development of a Conceptual Framework*, JCT/RIBA publications.

McGregor, W. and Shiem-Shin Then, D. (1999) *Facilities Management and the Business of Space*, Arnold.

Mackinder, M. and Marvin, H. (1982) *Design: Decision Making in Architectural Practice*, BRE Information Paper, Ip 11/82, July.

Nutt, B. (1993) 'The Strategic Brief P', *Facilities Magazine*, Vol. 11, No. 9.

Nutt, B. (1988) 'Strategic Briefing', *Long Range Planning*, Vol. 21, No. 4.

Office of Science and Technology (1995) *Progress through Partnership*, The Construction Board, HMSO.

O'Reilly, J. J. N. (1992) *Better Briefing Means Better Buildings*, The Department of the Environment/Building Research Establishment.

Parasuraman, A., Zeithaml, V. and Berry, L. (1985) 'A Conceptual Model of Service Quality and its Implications for Future Research', *Journal of Marketing*, Vol. 49.

Pennington, D. C. (1986) *Essential Social Psychology*, Arnold.

Peters, T. (1987) *Thriving on Chaos*, Panbooks.

Porter, T. (2000) *Selling Architectural Ideas*, E & FN Spon.

Preiser, W. (1993) *Professional Practice in Facility Programming*, Van Nostrand Reinhold.

Richardson, B. (1996) *Marketing for Architects and Engineers*, E & FN Spon.

RIBA (1993) *Strategic Study of the Profession, Phase II: Clients and Architects*, RIBA publications.

RIBA (1995) *Strategic Study of the Profession, Phases 3 and 4: The Way Forward*, RIBA publications.

Salisbury, F. (1998) *Briefing Your Architect*, The Architectural Press, 2nd edition, reprinted by Butterworth Heinman.

Salisbury, F. and White, B. (1980) *Briefing and its Relationship to Design: Draft Guide for Clients of the Construction Industry*, Building Research Establishment.

Sanoff, G. (1977) *Methods of Architectural Programming*, Hutchinson & Ross.

Somogyi, A. (1999) *The Role of Project Management*, Report, unpublished.

Spedding, A. (1994) *CIOB Handbook for Facility Management*, Longman Scientific and Technical.

The Tavistock Institute (1999) *The Role of the Architect in the Supply Chain*, Draft Workshop Report.

University of Bath Management School (1998) *Building*, Report of Study for Ballast Wiltshier, 21 August 1998.

University of Reading Centre for Strategic Studies (1989) *Investing in Building 2001*, University Of Reading.

Usmani, A. and Winch, G. (1993) *The Management of a Design Process: The Case of Architectural and Urban Projects*, Bartlett Research, Paper No. 1.

Walker, A. (1989) *Project Management in Construction*, Blackwell Scientific Publications.

Young, S. (1999) *Alternative Work Practices: Potential Implications for the Organisation, its Staff and the Physical Workplace*, MSc Report UCL, unpublished.

Zeisel, J. (1984) *Inquiry by Design*, Cambridge University Press.

Journals

Building Design
Building
Architects Journal
Facilities
Faculty of Building Journal
Journal of Marketing
Long range Planning
Quality Progress

Index